Mr Hill's Big Picture

Remembering James J. Fowler

Mr Hill's
Big Picture

The Day that Changed Scotland Forever –
Captured on Canvas

JOHN FOWLER

SAINT ANDREW PRESS
Edinburgh

First published in 2006 by
SAINT ANDREW PRESS
121 George Street, Edinburgh EH2 4YN

Copyright © John Fowler, 2006

10-digit ISBN 0 7152 0823 3
13-digit ISBN 978 0 7152 0823 6

The painting of the Disruption by David Octavius Hill is reproduced with permission of the
Free Church of Scotland, The Mound, Edinburgh. The author gratefully acknowledges this
permission.

British Library Cataloguing in Publication Data
A catalogue record for this book is available from the British Library.

Typeset by Waverley Typesetters in Bembo
Printed and bound by Bell & Bain Ltd, Glasgow

Contents

Key to picture

Thomas Chalmers	Hero of the Disruption, though a reluctant schismatic.
Hugh Miller	Stonemason, geologist, writer; eloquent voice of the Free Kirk.
D. O. Hill	He painted the picture.
Robert Adamson	Gifted early photographer; D. O. Hill's right-hand man.
David Welsh	On the day, played John the Baptist to Thomas Chalmers.
Robert Candlish	Firebrand; sponsored Hugh Miller, then fell out with him.
Ann Hill	Hill's first wife. She died young, before the Disruption.
Sir David Brewster	Eminent experimental scientist. He introduced Hill to Adamson.
Thomas Hately	Precentor (praise leader). Sang to the Lord with cheerful voice.
Mrs Anne Hanna	Chalmers' eldest daughter – Roman Catholic tendencies were alleged.
George Bell	Doctor friend of Hill; concerned observer of Edinburgh low life.
Alexander Black	Professor of theology, pilgrim to Palestine (hence the open atlas).

Dhanjiobai Naurojie   Parsee convert, later evangelical missionary in India.

James Young Simpson   (later Sir James) of chloroform fame; professor of midwifery.

Sergeant Mackenzie   Free Kirk officer; pipe major of the Black Watch at Waterloo.

Maitland Makgill Crichton   Laird, long-distance walker, called 'the poor man's friend'.

Thomas Burns   More pious than his uncle, the poet Robert. Minister of the Kirk.

Sir George Harvey   Painter, president of the RSA; friend and mentor of D. O. Hill.

Adolph Saphir   As a boy, the Kirk's first Jewish convert in eastern Europe.

Patrick MacFarlan   Seen signing away his livelihood, the richest living in the Kirk.

Henry, Lord Cockburn   Judge, friend of D. O. Hill, diarist.

Mrs Grace Chalmers   Wife of Thomas.

James Flucker   Newhaven fisherman.

William Cunningham   Theologian – 'big, combative, irascible'.

Lyman Beecher   American observer; father of Harriet Beecher Stowe.

Dr Merle d'Aubignon   Of Geneva. One of several Free Kirk sympathisers from abroad.

Hugh Mackenzie   Minister at Tongue. A martyr to the cause.

John Henning   Hill's elderly sculptor friend – implausibly sconced in a skylight.

DOH & ARH   Initials on chairback – for Hill and his second wife Amelia.

1

Picture on the wall

What picture? (you may ask)
– That *famous* picture. The Disruption picture.
Ah. (Pause) Tell me about it.

Stand by the Scott Monument in Princes Street, Edinburgh, all encrusted with grimy statuary, gargoyles and gothic curlicues, and look across the public gardens and the railway to the ridge of the Old Town rising towards the castle. In one of the frowning buildings that front the ridge – known as Presbytery Ridge to the initiated – hangs Mr Hill's big picture.

It's not readily seen, though the colonnaded National Gallery of Scotland is only a few hundred yards away, on the man-made causeway known as the Mound. A stranger might expect to find the picture displayed there, considering that it illustrates a climactic event in Scotland's relatively recent history, and that it was painted by one of nineteenth-century Scotland's most reputable artists. Or, more appropriately, perhaps, it could be housed in the Scottish National Portrait Gallery in nearby Queen Street.

But the painting is in private hands. It belongs to, and is cherished by, a branch of the Scottish Kirk whose past it celebrates, and it hangs in the great hall of the Free Church college, a room of astonishing elegance considering its dour immediate surroundings. Few people know of the picture's

1

whereabouts, if they have heard of it at all, and those who do must apply for permission to view it.

A recent visitor might have seen the author of this book mounted on a step ladder and inspecting the canvas – twelve feet wide and nearly five feet high, in a ponderous gilt frame – with a magnifying glass in his hand. There he could be seen peering closely at details invisible from the floor, searching in the tiniest brushstrokes for the hand of the master.

There is a lot to catch the eye. The picture shows more than 450 men and women crowded together – only a few are shown full length – and all are likenesses of people identifiable in their day. Who were they, and why are they there? I recognised only a few, not more than a handful; but in time, as I got to know them better, they began to seem almost like old friends.

'It is alive and arrests', a newspaper critic wrote when the picture was unveiled some 150 years ago. But is it now, and does it still? Not obviously; the subject is essentially static with no lively action to quicken the interest. So many faces, row upon row, and so few of them recognisable today! A plum duff of the forgotten and unknown – or, perhaps, a crammed page from a giant Victorian scrapbook.

David Octavius Hill was forty-one years old when he began his Disruption picture, and sixty-four when he finished it. It was to have been his masterpiece but, somehow, over the years, it got out of hand and latterly became to seem more like his grand folly. The drama is less in the picture than in the making of it, and in the events that lay behind it.

Hill was a gifted painter of landscapes in his day, but not of portraits. He had a gently romantic line in scenes of sunlit water, feathery woodland, craggy rocks and distant hills, with possibly a cottage, castle or ruined abbey in the middle distance. Figures in the landscape were usually secondary – milkmaids, laundresses, peasants and sometimes casual gentlefolk.

Yet, for his Disruption picture he deserted the natural world to represent a throng of figures jostling elbow to elbow in the drabbest of indoor settings. Mainly, he concentrated on their faces.

It wouldn't be true to say that he painted from life; but it was the next best thing. He took photographs. That is to say, he collaborated with a talented photographer named Robert Adamson to produce a series of portrait negatives which he used as a guide for the characters in his painting. Their work together has earned the partnership of Hill and Adamson worldwide fame as pioneers in the art of photography. Since then, many artists have used photographs as an aid, to a greater or lesser extent, not always successfully and not always admitted. Hill was the first to do so.

The year is 1843, and the talk of the nation is the great Disruption in the Church of Scotland. It's not an event much remembered today, except by a few, mostly historians or church-goers aware of their past. But it was a fierce controversy at the time. It caused a violent split within the established national church in an age when religion was the anchor as well as the opium (as Karl Marx called it that year) of most of the people. The Disruption divided society sharply; it embittered relationships and created long-lasting hostility. And it roused interest far beyond Scotland. In a word, it was a great schism.

It was not the first and it would not be the last division in the Kirk. Scots Presbyterianism has always been a contentious faith, prone to splinter into a tangle of seceding fellowships, sometimes with strange-sounding names like Burghers and Anti-Burghers, Auld Lichts and New Lichts. (It's the last you will hear of them in this narrative.) But still the Church of Scotland – the Auld Kirk – held to its course as the national Church established by law, recognised as a pillar of the Scottish nation along with the courts and the educational system, and guaranteed in the Union. The shock delivered by the Disruption was greater than all previous secessions put together.

Hill was an ardent supporter of the Disruption and of the men – they were almost exclusively men – who brought it about. The Evangelicals, as they were known, were men of fervent and puritanical faith, in marked contrast to the more easy-going Moderates who had hitherto held sway in the Kirk. Hill had many Evangelical friends. Recognising that the Disruption was a turning point in history – and since this was an age of historical painting – Hill determined to commemorate it on canvas on a suitable scale. At the outset, Hill made the rash forecast that the picture would be finished within three years. He had a hard lesson to learn. It took him twenty-three.

You see the picture and gasp. So many *people*, real people. The overall impression – at least in reproduction – is sombre. This is deceptive, since the original is surprisingly colourful, given that a lot of the characters are dressed in black.

And there's a sunbeam, too, which has a symbolic significance. Rays of light stream down from an unseen opening in the ceiling, catching the straggling white locks of a man who stands with a Bible open before him, and spilling on to a figure below who bends over a table with a quill pen in his hand.

The man above him is Thomas Chalmers. Short of stature, broad of brow, his face pock-marked (though the pits have been masked by the painter's brush), Chalmers is the true hero of the piece: the uncrowned king of Scotland. The man below, a lesser figure, is signing away his livelihood – more of that later.

Only the men seated in the front row are shown full length. To the right of centre sits Hugh Miller, a labouring man turned savant, a geologist vexed by the mysteries of creation, a writer of grace, the voice – through the newspaper he edits – of the great collective assembled here. There are flowers at his feet, and copies of his journal.

For the moment, we may pass over the faces in the crowd, with these exceptions. One perhaps – that frail old man with averted eyes, smiling gently. Hugh Mackenzie hasn't long to live. He'll earn the name of martyr.

Two more. A thin, dark-haired young man cradling some kind of box in his hands – it's one of the earliest cameras. He is Robert Adamson, genius of the photographic art, who looks down – so it seems – at the focusing aperture. His presence is fanciful; he wasn't there on the day. Just above his head is his partner David Octavius Hill – a manly face with keen alert eyes, framed with golden hair. All *he* required was a sketch pad.

The wordy caption carved on the heavy frame, *The First General Assembly of the Free Church of Scotland. Signing the Act of Separation and Deed of Demission, at Tanfield, Edinburgh. May 1843*, never caught on as a title – not surprisingly. Even before the painting was finished, it was being referred to simply as the *Disruption Picture*, and so it remained.

At the Disruption, well over 450 ministers quit the Church of Scotland on a point of principle, alleging oppression by the government and courts of law – an act of defiance which had severe consequences for many of them, since it meant giving up their livelihood, quitting their homes and leaving their churches. Where ministers led, the people followed.

Sometimes there was real hardship, especially in the country-side. Hostile landowners made it difficult for the outed ministers and their families to find a home, and refused them anywhere to hold public worship. So they preached in the open air, on the seashore, in the fields, in barns or other makeshift shelters. Many were ostracised by the ruling aristocracy, the gentry, the lairds, who wielded considerable power (at least in rural districts) over the lives of the people. Feelings ran high, and old friendships were broken. But they made a Church, a *Free* Church, which flourished and prospered.

Memories of the Disruption remained strong into the twentieth century. It has been called a watershed, a turning point, the greatest single event in Scotland in the nineteenth century – and a tragic mistake.

2

Farewell to Egypt

The great excitement which has prevailed in town since the beginning of the week was yesterday increased to the utmost intensity. Thousands arrived from all parts of the country on Wednesday, and during the morning of yesterday; and from an early hour, the crowded state of the streets showed that something of wide-spread, all-engrossing interest was about to take place.

Hugh Miller in the *Witness*, 19 May 1843

The crisis came on Thursday, 18 May 1843, in Edinburgh. No one knew how it would turn out. Would the great Schism take place after all? Would it fail? Would there be trouble in the streets?

A few knew the answers, or thought they did. John Hope, Dean of the Faculty of Advocates, the most influential lawyer in Scotland and a bitter foe of the Evangelicals, was contemptuous. He made a sneering calculation on his fingers. When it came to the crunch, he said, only half a dozen malcontents – ten at the most – would leave the fold and abandon the established church. Others said twenty, thirty, forty, not more. And the snell wind of poverty would soon bring them to their senses. They'd slink back.

John Crichton Stuart, Marquis of Bute, agreed. He'd guaranteed as much in high places. Lately he'd assured the prime minister Sir Robert Peel and his cabinet that only a handful of hot-tempered men would stick to their principles and go. It would be a non-event. Bute, a man of immense wealth, with estates in the Isle of Arran, Wales and elsewhere, had been appointed the young Queen Victoria's representative at the General Assembly of the Kirk in Scotland and, as Lord High Commissioner, had taken up residence in her official Scottish home at Holyrood Palace. Over dinner, when the talk turned to ecclesiastical matters, he'd been complacent. (For his pains, he would be made a Knight of the Thistle.)

The correspondent of the *Scotsman*, Edinburgh's influential newspaper, who had inside knowledge, was categorical. 'We have been informed upon what we esteem good authority that there will be no disruption in the church.' The government, he understood, would settle the affair with a judicious bill and 'the ensuing general assembly will be one of the quietest we have had for some time'.

Wrong.

The Assembly, the annual meeting and supreme court of the national Church – the Auld Kirk, as it was affectionately known among its adherents – took place every spring, attended by representative parish ministers and elders.

Many faced an arduous journey. The roads in most places were not good, and travellers faced a jolting journey by horse and coach or gig. Where possible, a voyage down the coast by sailing vessel might be preferable. Railways, as yet, could benefit only a few. The line between Glasgow and Edinburgh had opened only the previous year (stopping at Haymarket, short of Princes Street – Waverley was still to come).

The Rev. Adam White had one of the most arduous journeys. He had to make his way from North Ronaldsay, one of the outlying Orkney islands; and, by 19 May, the day after the Assembly began, he had got no further than Kirkwall on the Orkney mainland. Once he arrived in Edinburgh, he would probably be put up by wellwishers: friends of the movement had been asked to provide hospitality, and it was reported in the *Witness* newspaper that a subscription had been opened to defray expenses 'as the brethren are, in very many instances, put to great expense in travelling from the most distant parts of the country to the metropolis'.

One at least came from much further. Robert Walter Stewart was in Constantinople when he learned that the Disruption was inevitable. Determined to be there, he set out post-haste across Europe and made it to Berwick on the eve of the big day. From there he travelled overnight by road, since the rail connection with Edinburgh had not yet been made, arriving in the city at four in the morning – in time to take breakfast and hasten to join his friends.

Two men were present in the city waiting to record the occasion, each in his own way. One was the journalist Hugh Miller, self-educated stone mason turned geologist and then writer, a man instantly recognisable by his great flamboyant crown of red hair and the shepherd's plaid slung round his broad labourer's shoulders. He observed the crowds milling around him in the city streets – it had been like that for the best part of the week – and made ready to describe the scene in print for an avid readership.

The other, David Octavius Hill, was almost as noticeable a figure as Miller, with his flowing blond locks and dashing air. His representation of these great events or, at least, one incident among them, would take considerably longer than Miller's to reach the public eye.

It was going to be a day of pageantry. The sight of horse soldiers drawn up in double line along the High Street made Hugh

Miller uneasy. It reminded him of past days when the king's dragoons had sabred Covenanters on the moors.

'As the morning wore on, crowds thickened in the streets', he wrote. People had been about almost from break of day. The earliest risers were seen hastening to secure a place in the elegant church of St Andrew, in the New Town, where the Assembly was to be convened.

For the chief participants, the first event of the day took place at Holyrood, where a reception, or levee, was given by Lord Bute in his capacity as Lord High Commissioner. As was customary, it was attended by the great and the good, 'a large attendance of noblemen and gentlemen, naval and military officers' (a happy conjunction of church and state), who packed elbow into elbow in the state rooms. Prominent among the guests was General Sir Neil Douglas, commander-in-chief of the forces and a veteran of Corunna and Waterloo. Lower down the social scale were the civic dignitaries in their swishing robes. And kirkmen were there, of course, soberly dressed in ecclesiastical black, including leaders of the Evangelical party such as Dr David Welsh, currently Moderator of the Church of Scotland, the elder statesman Thomas Chalmers, and Robert Candlish, a coming man. All peaceable men of the cloth, you would say, though not gathered there in perfect amity, as the day would show.

Shreds of morning mist lifted from the high tenements of the Old Town, and stray glints of sunshine broke through, glancing on the drawn swords of the dragoons on the approach to St Giles. Other troops were lined up in the courtyard of Holyrood at the foot of the Royal Mile – more dragoons and a guard from a regiment of foot, clad in scarlet. Carriages waited there for the levee to end; horses champing and stamping on the cobbles, harness jingling; the occasional whiff of horse droppings.

Indoors, there was a small mishap. A bottleneck formed as guests pressed forward to be presented to Lord Bute in the throne room, and some were pushed against the walls. Miller reported: 'Suddenly – whether brushed by some passer-by, jostled rudely aside, or merely affected by the tremor of the floor – a large portrait of William the Third, that had held its place in Holyrood for nearly a century and a half, dropped heavily from the walls'. Thus King William, whose accession had secured the Protestant succession and established the rights of the Kirk of Scotland, hit the floor. A voice rang out: 'There goes the revolution settlement!' It was a moment, thought Miller, that 'history, though in these days little disposed to mark prodigies and omens, will scarce fail to record'.

At a little past noon, Lord Bute and his entourage issued from Holyrood to make their way to the High Church of St Giles for the church service that preceded every Assembly. Trumpets brayed, silvery notes bouncing from sandstone walls and granite setts; the band struck up *God Save the Queen*. A long procession formed: magistrates accompanying the Lord Provost in his finery, the city sword and mace in a separate coach; six trumpeters in gaudy state dress; Lord Bute with his chaplain and purse-bearer in the state carriage drawn by six horses, flanked by a dozen yeomen of the Scottish guard, six on each side; the general commanding in his coach; followed by nobles and 'private gentlemen' – including, presumably, ministers and elders – some in carriages, others walking, with another detachment of dragoons somewhere in the middle of them.

This pageant, as the *Scotsman* described it, made its cumbrous way towards the London road, crossing the low ground soon to be occupied by the lines of the North British Railway – the link with Berwick and London was planned but not yet built. To the martial sound of trumpet and drum, it wound round the base of Calton Hill, watched by dense crowds on its slopes. Robert Adamson, lately arrived from St Andrews and now in residence in a house on the hill, may have been among them. David Octavius Hill, living further away in Inverleith Row, maybe not. Calton Hill was then still relatively naked, almost rural in the heart of the city; its grassy bank was much used as a laundry green. It had recently been topped by a screen of classical columns intended to be a national monument, but never finished; they stand there yet, a diminished parthenon.

Miller was unimpressed by the show: 'There was much bravery and glitter – satin and embroidery, varnish and gold lace – no lack, in short, of that cheap and vulgar magnificence which can be got up to order by the tailor and the upholsterer for carnivals and Lord Mayor's days'.

It passed the Jail and the Bridewell (both houses of correction now replaced by St Andrew's House, where civil servants have their desks), the Calton cemetery (still there) and the long-gone cattle market, before turning on to the North Bridge to cross into the High Street. At a quarter to one o'clock precisely, the Lord High Commissioner's coach reached St Giles, where Lord Bute alighted and entered the dim interior of the venerable kirk.

After the pageantry, the preaching. Dr Welsh in the pulpit, a pale figure, with the Bible open before him at St Paul's epistle to the Romans: 'Let every man be fully persuaded in his own mind'. He was persuaded, for one. 'The eyes of all Christendom must be attracted to our struggle', he said. A question might be posed: 'Should we not yield to the wishes of earthly superiors?' No – 'We cannot yield what conscience claims'. Rather than seek the peace of the world, 'say rather with Christ, the cross, the cross! Thrice blessed tree, there is no wood like thine.'

This elevated invocation chimed with the hopes, and the fears, of those who were about to follow him into the unknown. Those who were not wriggled in the pews.

St Andrew's church in George Street is the very symbol of polite Georgian Edinburgh (it was built in 1784 to serve the bourgeoisie in the mansions of their fine New Town). A slender spire, chastely decorated, points heavenwards above plain curving walls and a pillared portico. You see it now as it was then, though a little more grimed with time.

'By four o'clock in the morning, eager spectators had begun to fill the church', wrote the Victorian novelist Margaret Oliphant in her biography of Thomas Chalmers. The *Witness* agreed: 'The public gallery was filled to overflowing at an early hour – many, principally ladies, having been there so soon as at four or five o'clock in the morning'. The *Scotsman*, more cautiously, reported that 'not a few' of the seats had been occupied since seven. Entrance was by ticket only, and Miller reckoned that ten times as many were disappointed, 'great numbers, even of ministers and elders, being unable, owing to the crowded state of the building, to obtain admission'.

The crush, outside and in, became almost intolerable as the morning wore on and more and more people tried to push their way inside, 'rendering the position of those standing inside anything but agreeable'. Long before proceedings got under way, the gallery was crammed and all seats designated for the public in the pews and boxes below were occupied. 'The whole house was filled from floor to ceiling.' It was standing room only.

In contrast, the central area set aside for the ministers and elders chosen to represent their local presbyteries in that year's Assembly remained empty throughout the morning. This railed-off horseshoe of pews brought to mind a political debating chamber, and the resemblance was apt. A single aisle divided the seating into left and right. On the left would sit the 'Evangelicals', the keepers of the Covenanting flame, the hotheads, the 'Wild' as they were sometimes called. On the right, the 'Moderates', inheritors of Enlightenment ideals, for whom zealotry was anathema and the status quo sacred. And there were cross-benches, too, for the few who shilly-shallied.

As the clock ticked towards noon, a trickle of Moderates began to take their seats, followed by more, until Miller was able to observe that 'very few of the Moderate party appeared to have been hearing the Moderator's sermon, as they were almost all in their places in St Andrew's Church before it was finished in the High Church'.

One of the earliest to arrive was the Moderate leader Dr George Cook, professor of moral philosophy at the University of St Andrews and historian of the Reformation, who stalked in about half-past twelve and stood nonchalantly under the eyes of the onlookers 'conversing, to all appearances very heartily, with his friends as they came in'. Not all Moderates were as jovial as he. Two were seen sitting together lost in thought and 'talking to nobody'.

At last the St Giles contingent made their appearance, threading their way through the mob clustered at the doorway. Immediately there was a craning of necks inside, whispered recognitions and even a few unseemly shouts of encouragement. No doubt about it, the onlookers were partisan. Here came Dr Robert Smith Candlish ('loud and repeated burst of applause from all parts of the House') whose new, hastily built brick and wooden church stood ready to receive him at the top of Lothian Road if, or rather when, he had to quit his present charge. Some Moderates affected to be much amused at these demonstrations of support. Dr Cook's friend Mr Bryce, in particular, was seen to look around and about, smiling disdainfully the while.

At almost half-past three in the afternoon, Dr Welsh slipped in and took the chair, followed a few minutes later by the entry of Lord Bute, at which the whole gathering shuffled to its feet as he walked down the aisle to occupy the throne. This was set on a dais draped, swagged and canopied like an oriental potentate's tent, under a panel bearing the lion-and-unicorn emblem. 'The lord advocate, the lord provost of the city, the commander of the forces, and a crowd of other distinguished personages, civil and military, not unmingled with the gentler sex, thronged every inch of the space around the throne' – this from a contemporary history of the Disruption. As a backdrop to this crowded scene stretched the bare stone wall of the church, pierced by a single row of plain, rounded windows admitting the clear, unfiltered, Presbyterian light of day.

Dr Welsh's opening prayer – 'much disturbed' by confusion at the door, especially in the lobby – was followed by the entrance of Chalmers and some of his colleagues whose way had been blocked by the crowd outside. They went to their seats on the left amid a storm of applause, after which Welsh resumed. 'Fathers and brethren', he began, in the usual Assembly form of address. He had a document in his hand – a lengthy formulation of grievances against interference in spiritual affairs by the courts of law and the state. This indictment became known simply as the Protest. Its phraseology was dense and legalistic, from the opening 'We, the undersigned', followed by a 'Considering', and a 'Further considering' and a 'Considering further', and the enumeration of eight points, and a 'We therefore', and a 'Do protest' and a 'further protest', down to the 'And finally', the acknowledgement of 'our manifold sins, and the sins of the Church and nation' and at last to the declaration that 'we do for the purpose aforesaid withdraw accordingly'. It was a long time in the delivery but the whole congregation listened 'with breathless attention'.

When he had done, Welsh turned towards the throne above him, at which Lord Bute rose, looking flustered and distressed. Welsh bowed to him, then took his hat from the table, stepped down from the dais and walked to the door. Chalmers followed, and then, row by row, the whole Evangelical body stood and filed out, leaving the left-hand side of the arena deserted. Cheers broke out in the gallery, and its occupants got to their feet for a better view, some overcome with emotion. Once the disturbance was stifled, 'not a voice, not a whisper was heard': feelings ran too deep for words, according to an observer, who recorded that 'in very many, not female alone, but strong-minded men, it found vent in tears'.

Welsh, pale-faced, a slight figure, gowned, with his spindle legs encased in Moderator's gaiters, is about to leave our stage. He has not long to live.

The youngest of twelve children, a weak-chested country lad, he was born in a farmhouse near Moffat and 'named after the sweet singer of Israel', the psalmist David. He left for the High School of Edinburgh at the age of thirteen, and a year later entered the university. When he rather tardily became an ordained minister, he struggled to make a success of it, for he had 'little facility of utterance and preaching was always to him an oppressive labour', though it's said he was well enough liked by his parishioners. 'His bodily frame was but ill fitted to endure the laborious fatigue of his pastoral duties', and his 'peculiar shyness and reserve' made the offer of a chair at Edinburgh University attractive. By 1843, he had been professor of church history for twelve years.

He was one of the early sitters in front of Robert Adamson's camera. Several shots were taken, one of which Hill used as his model in the painting, where Welsh sits on the right hand of Thomas Chalmers, with a copy of the Protest in his hand. Welsh did not survive the Disruption long. When his health broke, he retired to his son-in-law's home at Helensburgh, where he failed, suffered bouts of violent pain, and died in April 1845.

Miller, preparing his copy for the press later in the day, told of the rolling applause and the forest of waving hats that greeted Welsh and Chambers and their supporters as they emerged into George Street and, with some difficulty, formed a straggling column. Women waved from the windows of the surrounding buildings and 'the very housetops were covered with groups of spectators' as they walked along, three or four abreast, with the crowd milling around, following in their footsteps or hurrying ahead, down Hanover and Dundas Streets, with the Firth of Forth visible below, to their destined meeting place at Canonmills.

It was a solemn band that followed Welsh and Chalmers into the unknown, and many had heavy hearts. But they found balm in a sense of righteousness. After all, they were accustomed to adopt the mantle of the Old Testament Hebrews – it was a common trope of the Evangelical pulpit. As a popular pamphlet of the time expressed it: *Farewell to Egypt*, subtitled *The Departure of the Free Church of Scotland out of the Erastian Establishment*. (Within a month 15,000 copies had been printed.) The seceders saw themselves, like the Israelites of old, as God's chosen people who now, freed from bondage, were about to enter Zion – Zion being, for the moment, a former gasworks by the Water of Leith.

3

O for Octavius

David Octavius Hill was forty-one years of age when the Disruption took place. He was an established artist and a well-known personality in the cultural life of Edinburgh. Almost everyone he met seems to have had a good word for him, captivated by his outgoing personality and boyish enthusiasms. Once he and Robert Adamson got together, he loved to pose for the camera, alone or with friends and colleagues. Try keeping him in the background! I think you can catch a glimpse of his character from the shots in which he appears.

You see him alone in a doorway, with one side of his face highlighted by bright sunshine, the other in deep shade, his white shirt cuffs folded back over his jacket sleeves in negligent fashion. Or standing in the same doorway with the tall William Borthwick Johnston. Hill puts an elbow matily on his friend's shoulder as they face the camera with a jaunty look.

In one rather fuzzy image, Hill, the devoted father, seats his little daughter Charlotte (called 'Chatty') on his knee, cradling her head fondly at his breast. It helped to hold the child steady, of course; but no matter, it was a loving gesture. Sometimes there's company, as with the threesome in a photograph called *Edinburgh Ale*. The trio are grouped at table obviously enjoying a glass of this notoriously heady brew. Hill has a wicked grin on his face. The other side of the coin is shown in sobering contrast in *The Morning After*, perhaps intended by Hill as a companion piece. The dishevelled artist sits with legs splayed,

18

hair tousled, head bent. One elbow rests on a side table with a carafe and a glass on it. Standing beside him, a severe-looking gentleman – in fact, a well-known surgeon – takes his pulse.

Hill enjoyed his glass – and sometimes more. He writes jocularly of a function at which too many healths were drunk, which he left 'with a splitting headache, having taken a roasted potato at dinner – the effects of which were not obliterated by seven or eight glasses of capital champain'.

Always with an eye for the evocative setting for a photograph, he marshalled friends in Greyfriars churchyard where the monuments and tombstones provided decorative accessories. There he experimented with different groups, posing with – among others – a gravedigger (real or supposed) and the artist Thomas Duncan. Other expeditions took him to Bonaly Tower, on the fringe of the Pentland Hills, home of the judge Lord Cockburn, where he joined host and other guests in outdoor tableaux. In one, he sprawls on the hillside among a picnic party.

Henry Cockburn was a great walker. 'There's a fellow very like him, who traverses the Pentlands in a dirty grey jacket, white hat, with a long pole', he wrote, describing himself. 'That's Cocky – a frivolous dog.' Frivolous maybe, but also a Kirk man, and a wary supporter of the Evangelicals in the great debate. Every year, Cockburn took friends on an expedition to a spot called Habbie's Howe in the Pentlands, where the 'hermit fare' might include cold veal, salmon grilled at their Scout-type fire, tea, coffee and a dram or two. There were other outings, Hill sometimes in the boyish company. One of those occasions is described by James Nasmyth, son of the painter Alexander Nasmyth and a great friend of Hill. Nasmyth, an engineer by profession but also an accomplished amateur artist, told how the party set off on foot from 'Bonnie Bonaly' in September sunshine, Henry Cockburn in the lead. Most of his guests belonged to the artistic fraternity, including the painters David Roberts, George Harvey, Clarkson Stanfield and James

Ballantine, and D. O. Hill himself. (Cockburn's invitation had been for 'a Hill day', by which he meant the Pentlands rather than the painter.) Nasmyth took his wife along, but no other ladies were mentioned; Hill had been a widower for a dozen years by then.

Off they set, boots ringing on the rising path. It was 'rather a toilsome walk' as they wandered far into the hills – or so Nasmyth says. Possibly they ascended Capelaw or the neighbouring hills. Wherever it was, they reached 'a favourite spot' where they caught their breath again in a hollow in the hillside, redolent with the perfume of wild thyme. 'Here endeth the first lesson', said Cockburn in pulpit style as he seated himself in the centre of the circle. The towers and spires of old Edinburgh lay before them, framed between Arthur's Seat and the castle, and beyond it the glittering waters of the Forth, with the blue hills of Fife in the distance. They enjoyed the view and the conversation before descending alongside a murmuring burn for dinner at Bonaly, with haggis on the menu and whisky to wash it down. Then back to their several homes by carriage or gig, or even Shanks' pony.

In the fashion of the time, Hill enjoyed dressing up: in one photograph, he appears in so-called 'tournament dress' as a medieval troubadour, with lute. The instrument may have been more than just a prop, though whether he could play it is not known. On the other hand, he could sing – and did so eagerly when the company requested: 'at the board he was always jovial, and sang a good song', as a professor friend recalled. The essayist John Brown, discussing a watercolour sketch by Hill in his critique of Ruskin's *Modern Painters*, wrote in the *North British Review* that it was 'as sweet and deep in its tones as his own voice'. Hill's love of Burns was partly inspired by his appreciation, as performer, of the poet's songs.

He was gregarious, and had a sunny nature and a gift for friendship; in a word, he was fun. In her biographical *The Personal Art of David Octavius Hill*, Sara Stevenson succumbs to his charm, finding him 'one of the rare historical figures whose company is unfailingly attractive'. John Brown referred to his 'rich versatile rapid, facile mind, crowded with thick coming fancies'.

He could sing and he could dance. One night, at a ball given by the painter William Allan (Hill's mentor) at his home, Hill waltzed so energetically that he dizzied his young partner, who begged him to stop. 'Just one more round', he insisted, whirling her off again. At this, she said, 'I fell in a faint and had to be carried or led into another room and laid on a bed'. The experience was, as she added enigmatically, and in italics, '*Quite interesting*'.

In the light of such levity, it seems strange that Hill should have felt comfortable with the Calvinism of the Kirk, and identified so closely with the Evangelicals. Yet he admired and was the good friend of many of those whom he painted in the Disruption picture. An obituarist wrote that 'he was a seriously minded Free Churchman of profound convictions'. Serious at times, maybe, but not solemn. Presbyterians could have fun. Hearts beat beneath the black broadcloth.

Hill didn't wear his faith on his sleeve, but it can occasionally be glimpsed. 'Poor little fellow,' he wrote of a child, the second in a family to find an early grave, 'he has been taken, with his little sister, where they both see the face of Christ.' As for Thomas Duncan's widow, after that dear friend had died painfully, Hill recorded: 'it is now her great support that the Saviour was with him in his dark hour – and that he is in glory'. In the prospectus for his Picture, when it was finished years later, he harked back to Disruption day and the presence of 'Him who spoke to the multitudes on the Mount, and now, here to the hundreds of homeless men who had that day given their all for Him'.

Hill was an eighth son – hence Octavius, a name he disliked. He claimed that it was misspelt on the register and should have been Octavus, as later engraved on his headstone in the Dean cemetery in Edinburgh. He signed his works simply D. O. Hill, which was the form he preferred. To close friends of his youth, he was Davie.

At the age of sixteen, he left his native Perth for Edinburgh to attend painting classes, and stayed there for the rest of his life. The first works he exhibited were three landscapes, shown in 1821 at the Royal Institution ('for the encouragement of the fine arts in Scotland'). The Institution had been established two years earlier by members of the Edinburgh élite. Hill had been busy: in the same year, thirty of his Perthshire scenes appeared in a six-part series of lithographs, to be bound in an album ('royal folio, price six shillings') and showing 'places, either celebrated for Picturesque Beauty or Antiquity'.

The illustration on the cover pictured the corner of a placid loch with a sailing boat in the background and a mountain top (more like an Alpine peak than a Highland ben) in the distance. A massive boulder fringed with vegetation occupies the foreground, with, carved on its face: *Sketches of Scenes in Perthshire, Drawn from Nature and on Stone by D. O. Hill, 1821.* And below: 'Published by Thos. Hill' – this being his father.

Unusually, the plates were printed by lithography – literally 'on stone'. This was a bold step for a young man still in his teens, for the lithographic process had been discovered barely twenty years earlier in Germany. In lithography, the artist traces – or draws directly – on to a smooth limestone block which is then dampened and inked. The ink sticks to the crayon but is repelled by the damp surfaces. When a sheet of paper is placed on the block and put under a press, an image of the drawing is transferred to the paper. With care, many copies can be made – and, of course, sold at a profit.

Lithography's soft outlines are part of its appeal. A delicate process, it continued to interest Hill throughout his life. In lithography, artistic skill could be happily married to the craft of print-making – a forerunner, in a way, of the collaboration which Hill would embark on with Adamson twenty years later.

The Edinburgh printer John Robertson produced the first three parts of Hill's Perthshire views, and then, after a short interruption, the remainder were run off by Charles Joseph Hullmandel in London. Why the change was made is not known. Perhaps Robertson fell out of favour with the Hills, father and son, because he interrupted the work to embark on a rival production, a set of four plates from sketches by the artist John Knox (a contemporary painter, not the preacher) showing 'Scotish [sic] scenery drawn upon stone'. It was a borrowing too far.

Hill painted swiftly; an observer watched him dash off a watercolour sketch 'in the fine frenzy of an hour'. His landscapes are gently pastoral, pleasing, sentimental interpretations of the natural world seen through the filter of romantic sensibility. This quality can be seen in his large painting from the same period, his view of *Perth from Boatlands*, now in Perth Art Gallery, in which the distant town is seen from a broad reach of the limpid River Tay. A small fishing boat is anchored on the shore; and a smack, sails barely touched by the zephyr, is being rowed downstream. With its wide sky and reflections on the water, it's a cool essay in the play of light, almost Turneresque in feeling. Much later, his widow, Amelia, remarked that 'a careful observation of the play of light characterises his painting', adding: 'and his photography'.

The father, Thomas Hill, was a bookseller and stationer in Perth where his miscellaneous stock, according to his adverts in the local paper, included washable paper hangings 'for drawing parlours and bedrooms', pianofortes, sheet music and Cumberland pencils. In 1824, Thomas, in partnership with an elder son, also Thomas, moved the business to Edinburgh, where he set up as publisher, stationer, bookbinder, music and book seller.

Another Hill sibling, brother Alexander, also removed to the capital, at first as head clerk for Blackwood the publisher (notably of *Blackwood's Magazine*, the influential quarterly), before striking out on his own in a new line. Alexander proceeded to make his mark in the Edinburgh art scene as a publisher and seller of fine-art engravings, eventually opening a gallery in Princes Street, nicely placed in proximity to the grand, porticoed new art gallery on the Mound (now the Royal Scottish Academy building). David Octavius and he shared interests, to their mutual benefit.

A decade after the publication of his Perthshire views, Hill began work on an ambitious project to illustrate scenes associated with Robert Burns or characters from his works. By 1834, he was touring, mainly in the west of Scotland, setting up his easel at Tam o' Shanter's grave, or in a mossy dell in Craigieburn Wood, or in a village square overlooking the River Nith with the Solway in the distance. The workload was punishing, but by 1840 he had completed seventy-two paintings which were then engraved and published in two volumes as *The Land of Burns*. A long introductory essay was contributed by John Wilson, editor of *Blackwood's Magazine* and a professor at Edinburgh University. Notes to the plates were written by Robert Chambers, an Edinburgh publisher and author whose book *Vestiges of the Natural History of Creation*, published anonymously, was to cause a great scandal, since it undermined Biblical certainties and in a sense prefigured Darwin.

The Land of Burns was a bestseller – it could hardly fail, with the Bard as its inspiration. But, in the course of his tours, Hill had suffered for his art. Much travelling was involved, getting from place to place by coach or on foot, with railway journeys only possible at the very end of the period, and then only on a very limited scale. West-of-Scotland weather could be unkind to a man sketching or painting out of doors – sure of a drenching now and then. He was, as Sara Stevenson points out, 'an early plein-air painter', and exposure seems to have affected his health. 'You have not come scatheless from the land of Burns and I deeply grieve that your accursed rheumatism should so have fettered your good right hand', a friend wrote. This may have developed into a chronic condition which Stevenson concludes 'hindered and frustrated his manipulative talents' – a handicap, to say the least, for an ambitious artist needing dexterity in his fingers.

Hill hoped that his paintings could be hung in a permanent gallery dedicated to Burns; but, regrettably, the plan fell through, and he had to be content with a showing of the Burns pictures at his brother Alexander's gallery at 67 Princes Street in the latter part of 1851. Alexander acted as agent for the sale of the paintings, many of which were afterwards lost when they were destroyed in a fire.

In the 1820s and 1830s Hill was heavily involved in book illustration. This was a growing market, with the artist providing paintings designed for the engraver. He was one of several leading artists – Landseer was another – to provide illustrations for the Waverley novels, and engravings from his paintings appeared in an edition of the works of James Hogg, the Ettrick Shepherd. The most assiduous and sought-after painter in this field, and the one able to command the highest fees, was the Englishman J. M. W. Turner, an artist revered by Hill. Turner made several sketching excursions in Scotland, starting in 1797, and was entertained by Scott at Abbotsford in 1831 when commissioned to illustrate Scott's *Poetic Works*.

But by no means all the engravings made from Hill's paintings were intended, or destined, to illustrate books. The connection with his print-selling brother Alexander ensured that his pictures were copied by engravers for sale in multiple copies – the common form of reproduction in his day. 'There is no Scottish artist so many of whose works have been engraved', according to a historian of Scottish art, writing of Hill in the early 1900s. It was, he suggested, a useful addition to his earnings, but might not have been to his advantage in the long run: 'The greater number were painted with this object in view, and consequently are less valuable as paintings than as subjects for interpretation by the engraver.'

In 1830, while sketching in the west of Scotland, Hill struck up a friendship with the civil engineer, James Miller. Miller commissioned him to record features on the railway line he was building between Glasgow and the iron-making town of Garnkirk in north Ayrshire, and brother Alexander arranged for the illustrations to be lithographed for a souvenir edition. In Miller, Hill found a sympathetic patron as well as friend. In time, Miller came to own eight paintings by Hill, one of which, the *Braes o' Ballochmyle*, was a dramatic representation of the high-arched railway viaduct that Miller designed to span a river gorge in Ayrshire. A drifting wisp of steam from an unseen locomotive in the distance is Hill's only nod in the direction of the industrial age. Among the paintings that Miller commissioned is one of Hill's most successful panoramas, *Old and New Edinburgh, from the Mons Meg Battery*, which was later seen at an exhibition of the Royal Scottish Academy – a quarrelsome institution whose lifelong servant Hill had become.

The Scottish Academy, as it was called at first, had had a difficult birth. Before its existence, Scottish artists had struggled to get their work seen. Exhibitions had been held in Edinburgh since 1819 by an organisation called the Royal Institution, which showed a distinct preference for old masters and, failing that, for the more recently dead. To be Scottish and still painting was not a great advantage; Hill had done well to have had his journeyman landscapes shown. Wealthy patrons keen to exhibit their latest old-master acquisitions held sway, and practising artists had no say in what went up on the walls.

When the Institution moved into a splendid neo-classical building, provided for it on the south side of Princes Street by government money, many of the leading artists took the opportunity to break away and form a Scottish Academy more in keeping with their democratic spirit. Hill and some others dithered and held back. At first, they toyed with the idea of setting up a rival academy; but that didn't last long. A meeting held under the chairmanship of the venerable William Allan to constitute the new organisation broke up in disarray, possibly provoked by a boisterous intervention by Hill during a long-winded speech. Perhaps he had dined well.

In the end, the dissidents swallowed their pride and joined the existing academy, where they were civilly if not wholeheartedly welcomed. Their passage was eased by the advocacy of John Hope, at that time solicitor general in Lord Grey's government and a powerful man in Scottish legal circles. He would soon enter the great religious debate in virulent opposition to the Evangelicals. Hill proved popular with his colleagues, and, when the secretary resigned in 1830, he was offered the post. He accepted reluctantly, possibly because the job was unpaid and the duties onerous – the secretary being in present-day terms the administrator. The outgoing secretary complained of the sacrifice he had made: 'I cannot estimate my loss at less than £200 a year'. A further disincentive for Hill may have been that he was thinking of marriage, and the prospect of an extra financial burden would not be attractive.

Five years later, he did get on the payroll. His salary was never enough to live on, but it enabled him to marry Ann Macdonald, of whom little is known except that she, too, came from Perth, was the daughter of a wine merchant there, and was a pleasing musician. There was joy and sorrow. Charlotte was born in the first year of their marriage, and Hill adored her. Then a second daughter died hours after her birth. Ann fell ill and her songs ceased. She died when Chatty was three, in 1841, two years before the Disruption. But when Hill came to make his picture, she lived again: he painted her, a sad lady, in half profile, lifting her eyes to heaven.

Soon after Hill took up his post, he set about preparing the academy's fifth annual exhibition. It had been decided to add lustre to the young institution by asking some of Britain's leading painters to contribute pictures. To this end, Hill despatched a series of respectful letters in his almost indecipherable handwriting – his 'well known *illegible* hand', as a friend described it, a dashed-off characterless scrawl surprisingly careless in an artist. The recipients included Constable, Turner, Landseer and Sir David Wilkie – by then living in London, and considered to be the most successful artist of the time.

'With a view to stimulate the exertions of native Artists and advance the knowledge of Art in Scotland,' Hill wrote floridly to Constable, the academy was 'most anxious to be enabled to exhibit to the public of Edinburgh, fine specimens of the works of the most eminent British painters.' He hoped that Constable might contribute 'one or more of these triumphs of your pencil which have so often excited the admiration of many members of our Institution on their visit to the Metropolis'.

To Turner he wrote in even more ingratiating manner, 'with much deference and without having any claim on your good offices', adding that all expenses of carriage 'whether by Sea or land' would be defrayed. Alas, no picture by Constable or Turner materialised, though Turner did contribute to a later exhibition.

The following year, Hill was luckier with Wilkie, to whom he confirmed in February 1831 that *The Highlander's Return to his Family* had arrived safely: 'I had it unpacked by a careful hand'. Hill felt impelled to add rather more than a formal acknowledgement, writing that

It is with profound respect that I venture to transcribe my own more than half suppressed emotions on studying the picture of calm contentment, of domestic endearments, of manliness, modesty, innocence, and grateful attachment. The feelings it awakens are not less intense, nor less delightful in

their intensity, than those called forth by the most touching
of our melodies or the most perfect Lyrics of our heart strung
land, while the exquisite art by which the conception is
embodied, furnishes a pleasure unknown to the mere lovers
of Song. The chord you have touched so delicately & yet so
masterly, will find a responsive echo in many a Scottish bosom
and will if possible enshrine the artist still deeper in the hearts
of his admiring countrymen ...

At which Hill halts as if aware that his rush of warm-hearted
enthusiasm may have offended propriety: 'I have to apologise
for having obtruded on you any matter unconnected with
my official duty'. But he, too, was an artist and a singer, not
a functionary. He was, as George Harvey, by then known as
Sir George and president of the academy declared on Hill's
death, 'impulsive and enthusiastic' by nature; and, at first 'but
imperfectly acquainted with business, he occasionally required
the qualifying regulation of cooler and more practical heads'.
No, Hill was not a desk man, though he acquitted himself well
as secretary for nearly forty years.

Hill was later able to tell Wilkie that *The Highlander's Return*
had 'formed the chief object of attraction in the Rooms'. The
frame had been 'sent off by Smack last week', and the canvas
would follow.

Not long after his appointment, Hill had a lucky escape.
He and other academicians were attending an auction of old
masters. The large upper room was overcrowded, and when a
beam gave way, spectators were pitched below. A carpet nailed
at one end acted as a chute, depositing the unfortunate art-
lovers in a pile, one on top of the other in a cloud of plaster
dust and a roar of falling rubble. Two people died and many
were hurt, but Hill was left standing on the rim and got away
unscathed.

In the early years of Hill's tenure, the academy went through
several traumas, some seriously threatening its existence.
Relations between it and the stuffier Royal Institution were

uneasy, exacerbated by the fact that the academy relied on the goodwill of the Institution to give space for its exhibitions. In 1844, by which time it had been awarded a royal charter and was now the Royal Scottish Academy, a spat involving the hanging of a picture soured relations between the academy and the influential Sir Thomas Dick Lauder. The picture, *Scene after a Wreck – Twilight after a Storm*, was hastily removed from pride of place to an obscure corner after several artists objected vehemently that it was a work 'of no visible merit' on seeing it at the private viewing. Unfortunately, it had been painted by Lauder's son, and Sir Thomas wrote in a rage to Hill. Though expressing his regard for 'so many instances of your polite attention towards myself', Sir Thomas petulantly returned his complimentary tickets, and a bitter correspondence ensued in which the academy was threatened with legal action for defamation. In the end, the three-year wrangle was smoothed over with the legal help of Henry Cockburn. As for Lauder junior's *Scene*, asking price £35, it remained in obscurity and was later sold for a tenner.

Artists can be temperamental, inclined to take affront at any suspected slight, and the hanging of their pictures was always a touchy subject. Even Hill's sunny good nature must have been tested at times. One of the minor disagreements arose when the actor-turned-artist Robert Ronald McIan wrote to Hill to complain that visitors who wanted to view his *Sketch for a Highland Funeral* must crane their necks to do so. McIan, who had quit the boards a few years earlier – he had success on the London stage in an adaptation of *Rob Roy* – is known to posterity only for his kilt-and-claymore series *The Costume of the Clans*, prints of which sell well to tourists. It happened that his wife also had a picture in the exhibition. She was the only female artist to be a member of the academy – honorary, in her case – for many years. The disgruntled McIan wrote to Hill: 'My dear Sir, In case anyone *should* ask the price of Mrs McIan's picture, she desires me to say it is 35 guineas. As my

'Highland Feud' has been exalted to grace the ceiling no one is likely to trouble me. May I ask you to tell me who were the 'Hangers' this season that I may at least thank them for hanging my wife's picture well.' Whether Hill managed to soothe McIan is not known.

By 1843, Hill had survived all trials for a dozen years and had consolidated his position. The following year, as usual, he had several works of his own in the academy exhibition, including two landscapes lent by his friend and patron, the engineer Miller. But of particular interest were items numbered 550 to 557, described in the catalogue as *Calotype Portraits Executed by R. Adamson under the Artistic Direction of D. O. Hill*. These small photographic images, sepia in tone, light and dark, soft-edged and luminous, were strikingly original. Few had seen anything like them. They were enchanting.

Among the sitters portrayed were the artist Sir William Allan, an unnamed lady, the Rev. Julius Wood (of Dumfries and Malta), George Kemp – whose Scott Monument gothic folly was rising, stone by stone, hard by the Royal Institution building – and Sir David Brewster, scientist, encyclopaedist, communicator, principal of St Leonard and St Salvator colleges in St Andrews, and high priest of a new mystery, the fledgling art of photography.

4

Pleased to meet Mr Adamson

I got hold of the Artist, shewed him the Calotype, and the immense advantage he might derive from it in getting likenesses of all the principal characters. He was at first incredulous, but went to Mr Adamson.

Sir David Brewster to William Henry Fox Talbot, 3 July 1843

Bulldog Brewster, a difficult man; quick to take offence, not easy to live with, adept at losing friends. After years of hard work, too close to the edge of solvency for his liking, supporting his scientific explorations by means of his journalism, he had at last gained security on his appointment in 1838 as principal at the united colleges of St Leonard and St Salvator at St Andrews University. Within five years he had outworn his welcome.

'He lives in St Andrews and presides over its principal college, yet no one speaks to him!' wrote Henry Cockburn. 'With a beautiful taste for science, he has a stronger taste for making enemies of friends. Amiable and agreeable in society, try him with a piece of business, or with opposition, and he is instantly, and obstinately, fractious to the extent of something like insanity. With all arms extended to receive a man of whom they were proud a few years ago, there is scarcely a hand that he can now shake.' Another commented: 'Nobody ever had dealings with him and escaped a quarrel'. On the other hand, it was remarked that sometimes under his crabbed exterior, charm could be found.

When, as an elder of the Kirk and 'the very model of a Scottish Presbyterian', Brewster walked out with his friend Chalmers at the Disruption, professors at St Andrews who had been inconvenienced by his reforming zeal jumped at the chance to have him sacked, arguing the case that university appointments should be held exclusively by members of the established church. They failed to dislodge him.

It was not only his temper that was inflammatory. An experimental scientist rather than a theorist, he spent money (which he could ill afford), time and effort on his laboratory work, and suffered the occasional accident in the course of his chemical experiments. An explosion blinded him temporarily.

Troubled Brewster! Even in his profession as scientist ('philosopher' in the terminology of the age), he raised hackles. In the end, his principal optical theory would be found wanting, and he was snubbed by the Royal Society of London. He had, by the way, the curious notion that there might be intelligent life on other planets. By the early 1840s, in spite of his great talent, he could be described as embittered and a lonely outcast.

As a young man, Brewster had been frustrated in his first choice of career, the Church, by a strange disablement: unlike his three brothers, all parish ministers, he found he could not preach; and, since preaching the word was the essence of the Presbyterian ministry, this proved fatal to his hopes. What unmanned him in the pulpit is not quite clear. Some speech impediment has been suggested – stutter, lisp, Scots burr? Or a 'nervous faintness'? We don't know. There was some fatal lack of fluency, perhaps an inability to extemporise, a pathological fear of speaking in public, or of losing the thread or the place. At any rate, he found the experience too nerve-racking to persist in, and so he renounced the pulpit for the laboratory.

As a physicist, he made his name in the study of optics, making discoveries about the diffraction and polarisation of light. Such was his distinction in the field that it won him a knighthood, a clutch of medals including one from the Photographic Society of Paris in 1868, the year he died, and the commemoration of his name in the Australian plant *Cassia brewsteri* (a small tree), the mineral brewsterite, Cape Brewster in Greenland, and the brewster, a unit for measuring the reaction of optical materials to stress. He made his first telescope as a boy of ten, under the guidance of the ploughwright and self-taught maker of scientific instruments James Veitch, in his home town of Jedburgh. As a student at Edinburgh University, he shared his enthusiasm for optical experiments with an older contemporary, Henry Brougham, later a Lord Chancellor, with whom he maintained a friendship in spite of taking opposite sides in the great church controversy, and from whom he received influential support at turning points in his career. 'He is at the head of our men of science', Brougham wrote, much later. Today he is remembered, if at all, as the inventor of the kaleidoscope.

At St Andrews, it was natural that he should become involved with a small circle of academics and lay people struggling to achieve success in the newly revealed art of photography, the strange art of making pictures with light. He acted as their mentor, publicist and promoter.

The news had broken in January 1839 when the Frenchman Louis Daguerre published the results of his experiments resulting in the first permanent photographic image. The word 'camera' – literally, a chamber – was well known. Artists were familiar with the camera obscura and had long used it as an aid to drawing. Through a lens, it projected an image of the subject before it, say a landscape, which could be traced by the artist on paper. Of course, the image disappeared as soon as the aperture was closed and the light shut out. Daguerre's breakthrough was to discover a means of preserving that vanishing image.

His 'daguerreotypes' were black-and-white pictures printed on silvered copper plates, finely detailed, beautiful, shimmering and magical in their effect. They were works of art, a delight to the eye. The daguerreotype seemed to capture nature as it was, not as an artist interpreted it, fallibly. Nothing like it had been seen before. But, from our present point of view, there was a drawback. Each daguerreotype was unique and could not be reproduced. It was a precious one-off.

Meanwhile, the Englishman William Henry Fox Talbot, unaware of what was happening across the Channel, was working on his own photographic process (he called it the calotype process, from the Greek *kalos*, beautiful, and *typos*, image), quite different from Daguerre's. His great achievement was to discover how to make a negative from which any number of positive copies could be printed off.

Talbot, a country gentleman of independent means and scientific interests, botany in particular, was spurred on by envy of his cultured friends and relatives who were all reasonably accomplished amateur artists. To his dismay, he had no such talent. His mother, sister and wife could sketch, and he couldn't – he was shamed. He used to tell the tale, possibly enhanced by hindsight, of how this led to his pursuit of photography.

The year was 1833. He was on holiday at Lake Como in northern Italy – he and his bride accompanied by a half-sister and her husband. The others sketched happily away; but not he. Even when he squinted through a clever optical gadget called a camera lucida (really a prism, not a camera) and tried to copy what he saw, the results were poor. 'The faithless pencil had only left traces melancholy to behold.' All that can be said of his tentative view of Lake Como, now in the museum of photography at Bradford – showing terrace, trees, lake and hills – is that it's neat, precise and spidery, nothing more.

But he had a working knowledge of chemistry, knew about light-sensitive materials and, after much trial and error, found a way to imprint a permanent image on sensitised paper. It was a negative; the subject reversed from left to right, the tones from black to white. Others had reached that point, only to give up in frustration – who wants a ghostly travesty? But Talbot persisted and found a way to make positive prints on paper treated with various chemicals, including common salt. Hence these were known as salt prints. Daguerre's announcement spurred Talbot into rushing out the news of his own (at that time only partial) success.

Talbot had known Brewster for a decade. Brewster had been his house guest in Wiltshire, and they corresponded. Knowing Brewster's work on optics and his interest in photography, Talbot sent sample prints to St Andrews for his opinion. Brewster responded with enthusiasm, showing the 'numerous beautiful specimens of Photogenic Drawing' to friends and colleagues, one of whom, as he told Talbot, had been sent a sample of Daguerre's work from Paris – though 'yours excited a greater interest'. Brewster was so inspired by what he had seen that he ordered a camera obscura so that he, too, could try his hand, at the same time urging Talbot, if he would, to pass on the secrets of his success.

Talbot generously did so, though at first to no avail. Brewster dabbled but doesn't seem to have made more than a few attempts at hands-on photography himself. His role in the small St Andrews circle was to encourage, advise and provide a link with Talbot. Letters, progress reports, sped between them.

His ablest disciple in the St Andrews group was John Adamson. Adamson had qualified in medicine at Edinburgh and Paris before taking a spell as ship's surgeon in the China seas. On his return to St Andrews, he attempted to set up in practice as a family doctor, but found he was competing with too many medics for too few patients. So he occupied himself gainfully teaching chemistry and physics at Madras College school, joined a learned society which had been founded largely through the efforts of Brewster, and devoted himself to experimenting with photography. Brewster seems – for once – not to have fallen out with his new ally, and they remained friends.

Associated with them was an eminent son of St Andrews, later provost, Major Hugh Lyon Playfair, formerly of the Bengal artillery. His claim to fame as provost was that he cleaned up the town, which was none too salubrious at that time. Lesser lights were one Alexander Govan of Smith & Govan, chemists, South Street, Arthur Connell 'our Professor of Chemistry' and his assistant William Holland Furlong, Brewster's son Henry while briefly on leave from his duties as an infantry captain in Ireland and, while on a fleeting visit to St Andrews, Michael Pakenham Edgeworth, botanist son of Brewster's friend, the Irish novelist Maria Edgeworth.

At first, progress was slow and the results disappointing. Brewster to Talbot, July 1841: 'I have entirely failed in your Calotype process, and so have two of my friends, Major Playfair and Dr Adamson. Major Playfair has since tried it repeatedly and patiently by himself.' Too often, only a murky image appeared on the paper – 'Dr Adamson despairs'. Brewster plaintively sought help from Talbot: 'I shall wait anxiously. We need the very alphabet of the art.'

Talbot, steadily improving his technique, sent more examples to St Andrews, where they were well received: 'Major Playfair, Dr Adamson and myself are quite enchanted with the new specimens'. Brewster reported: 'My two friends are wholly absorbed in the subject, and having got the finest cameras ever made, they will never give up till they master the process'.

John Adamson's brother first appears in the record in 1842, when he was just twenty-one but already a rising star. Robert Adamson was a delicate young man. In a calotype of the Adamson family, he appears painfully skinny beside his healthier brothers – one of them in particular, the farmer of the family, exudes rude health. Robert's knees are bony, his face thin. His most striking features are a long, sharp nose and his quiff of thick dark hair.

Very little is known of Robert Adamson, whose life was too short, whose personality seems to have been too retiring to have left a mark, and whose talent was for too long overshadowed by the fame of his future partner, Hill. He was, as far as we can judge, sweet-tempered. He was brought up near St Andrews where his father farmed. A calotype image of the farm has survived, showing a plain stone farmhouse and steading in the traditional Scottish style, surrounded by clusters of conical haystacks – 'the youthful haunt of my amiable friend', as David Octavius Hill later wrote, treasuring the print, a mere scrap of paper.

The shy lad was ill-suited to farm labouring, and even less to the engineering work to which he was apprenticed as a youth. It has been speculated that his employer was John Annan, a millwright and flax-spinner at Dairsie in Fife; but there's no documentary evidence. His talent was clearly not for heavy work but for more intellectual pursuits, namely science and mechanics. He was good with his hands and he had an inventive streak, spending much time making working models including steam engines, the cutting-edge technology of the day.

Sometime in the early 1840s, young Robert was recruited as a willing apprentice to the St Andrews photographic cell. He learned fast and soon showed a remarkable aptitude for the tricky process. As his skill developed, Adamson made plans – or, perhaps, others were making plans for him. The camera might provide him with a living. 'A brother of Dr Adamson who has been educating as an engineer is willing to practise the Calotype in Edinburgh as a Profession', Brewster informed Talbot. 'I have twice discussed the matter with Dr Adamson and will let you know more particularly in a few days.' Talbot was assured that Mr Adamson had been 'well drilled' in the art by his brother, that his progress had been nothing short of brilliant and that he had now 'arrived at great perfection in the art'.

St Andrews in the mid-nineteenth century was a backwater despite boasting an ancient university. The town consisted of little more than three grassy streets converging on the skeletal ruins of an old cathedral, and its crowded fishing quarter was noisome and squalid. Edinburgh offered the chance of commercial success. Adamson moved to the city on 10 May 1843, finding both home and studio in the aptly named Rock House on Calton Hill. The imminent General Assembly of the Church of Scotland was probably not much in his thoughts, if at all. But, when the Assembly opened a week later, David Brewster was there as a representative elder of the Kirk, and David Octavius Hill was there sketching, with the idea of the great picture germinating in his mind. Brewster knew Hill – Brewster knew everyone! – and, when he spotted Hill at work with his pencil and pad, something clicked in his mind. What if the talents of the artist and his protégé photographer could be combined, to their mutual benefit? As he explained to Talbot, in the words quoted above, 'I got hold of the Artist, shewed him the Calotype, and the immense advantage he might derive from it in getting likenesses'. So he shepherded the reluctant Hill to a meeting with Adamson. The two talked, got on famously, and a partnership of genius was born.

5

At a stroke of the pen

We left Dr Welsh, gowned, capped, tasselled and gaitered, leaving the church of St Andrew's at the head of the godly phalanx. George Street was thronged – had been all morning – and for a moment there seemed to be no way through.

'One can feel the rustle yet hush of that crowd', wrote Margaret Oliphant, visualising the scene fifty years later (she had been a girl of fifteen at the time.) She continued:

> after a few minutes of breathless expectation a rustle of movement was heard, and the well known white head and pale impressive heavy countenance of Thomas Chalmers became suddenly visible, with the Moderator in his robes by his side, issuing from the door: and behind him an endless line, figure after figure, appearing like an army. The crowd held its breath, then breaking into tumultuous cheers, opened a narrow line in which three men could walk abreast, in the ever-lengthened line. No procession had been planned but the seceders were funnelled into a column by the press of bystanders, a dark and silent procession a quarter of a mile long which wound on between these living walls, recognized, shouted over, cheered with the wild outcries of unrestrainable emotion along the whole course of the way.

Eager supporters joined in on the way, so that, according to an eyewitness, the number marching swelled to more than 1,000.

Hugh Miller, in his report for that Friday's *Witness*, described how the 'tremendous burst of applause' in George Street 'was continued and reiterated with the most extraordinary enthusiasm as they went along. All the windows and staircases were filled with ladies … the very housetops were covered with groups of spectators – and the universal waving of hats and handkerchiefs from all quarters, mingled with the shouts below.'

Downhill they went through the streets of the New Town with the Firth of Forth and the hills of Fife lying in view before them, towards the northern outskirts of the city at Canonmills where they crossed the new bridge across the Water of Leith. All the way, crowds turned out to watch, or kept pace with them; but not in any tumult, as the *Scotsman* reported, for these onlookers were 'of different materials from the idle boys and trades-lads who constitute our normal street assemblages', embracing 'a large proportion of the most respectable merchants and professional men, and a very large number of well-dressed females'.

Thomas Hately, who sits in the very forefront of the picture, could only snatch a short break from his work at Constable the printers (his boss is also in the picture) to watch the marchers as they went by. Hately, as precentor, led the singing of psalms during the assembly, though he couldn't be present on the first day. He dashed along Thistle Street to catch sight of the procession at the street corner.

Canonmills had a rural aspect at that date. John Knox – the other John Knox – had set up his easel there some years before. His painting *A View of Edinburgh from Canonmills* shows washerwomen bleaching linen on the green beside the Water of Leith, the spot where the Tanfield premises would shortly be built. The scene as it was on Disruption day can be seen in an old engraving, after a painting by William Bonnar: handsome old trees shade the bridge across the water, and, on the far side, a black ribbon of people, stretching back into the distance, winds past the front of the Tanfield building – peculiarly oriental in appearance with pagoda-topped towers. A factory chimney is visible at the side.

The green field was first built upon in the mid–1820s when gas lighting was all the rage. Streets and homes in the centre of Edinburgh had been lit by gas for several years when the Oil Gas Company set up in Tanfield with what was claimed to be a superior manufacture – one that, unlike gas-making from coal, 'can never be a nuisance to the neighbourhood'. Sir Walter Scott, whose mansion at Abbotsford was lit by gas made from oil, was chairman of the company, and testimonials came from Dublin where gas made from oil had been successfully introduced. The project failed, the Oil Gas Company went out of business, and the Tanfield building was converted to other uses. The hall no longer exists. The site is occupied by commercial and financial offices, and the area has been engulfed by the growing city.

Hastily got ready when the Disruption seemed imminent, when it was described as the largest room in Edinburgh, Tanfield Hall could seat 2,500 and accommodate more than 3,000 with standing room. By the time Welsh and Chalmers and their followers arrived, to more hearty rounds of applause, the hall was already filled to overflowing with spectators – a 'large and most respectable company'. Hugh Miller sat on the press bench. It's likely that David Octavius Hill was present, though it's not possible to be certain. There is no record of what sanitary arrangements were made. The benches were hard, the overcrowded room stuffy, the proceedings lengthy. Somewhere at Tanfield there must have been the Victorian equivalent of the Portaloo. Earth closets, perhaps.

The surroundings were bleak and austere, unlike the elegant church they had left. It was a glorified shed. No matter; it became hallowed ground, and 3,000 heads bowed in prayer as Dr Welsh, his duties now almost at an end, called on the Lord to bless their actions that day.

Welsh has had a hard and deeply emotional day: first the overcrowded levee at Holyrood, then his sermon at St Giles, the ceremonial at St Andrew's church and the painstaking repetition of the protest document, the walk through milling crowds to

Tanfield, and now this. He is drained: 'In the exhausted state in which my numerous duties have left me, it is scarce in my power to say more', he begins. But, before quitting the chair, he must hand over to the 'one individual, whom to name is to pronounce his panegyric'.

He said the name. 'Dr Chalmers …' – and no sooner spoken than the whole gathering rose to its feet waving hats, hands and handkerchiefs, cheering wildly. No-one timed the acclamation, but they say it rang out for minutes on end. Hail to the hero!

Chalmers at sixty-three: a stocky man, broad-built, clumsy. (Once he fell off his horse.) His face was coarse, according to Lockhart, Scott's biographer. People remarked on the breadth of his brow, 'a mathematical forehead' as it was once curiously described.

Ponderous though his eloquence was, he knew how to sway a crowd. The report of his address is peppered with shouts of enthusiasm: 'Hear, hear!', 'Cheers!', 'Applause!' – and only once is there a hint of dissent: 'Some distant sounds of disapprobation', growls from the gallery when he failed to go far enough for the militants. The muttering was soon silenced.

He summarised the history of events leading up to the crisis. He recalled the tribulations of the Covenanting martyrs, he urged humility but no compromise – it was all to be expected. So was his belief in the necessity of an established church to uphold Christian faith and morals: 'We hold it to be the duty of government to give of their substance and means for the maintenance of religion in the land'. He ended with the words of a true Evangelical. They would hold fast to the Bible and their belief, like Paul and the apostles, in good times and bad; they should prepare for sacrifice. At that, he laid down his notes and took his seat. The audience approved; and their loud and sustained applause, as the *Witness* noted, rolled round the hall.

The *Scotsman* was unimpressed. Scathing, even. 'What a tissue of strange stuff it is!' a leading article commented – a 'farrago'.

> After leading his confiding followers to throw up their livings, and risk every worldly comfort for the 'Free Presbyterian Church', he seems now anxious to deprive them of the sympathies of those who would be most disposed to befriend them. The most bigoted Conservative, the most servile worshipper of aristocracy, could not utter sentiments more base and grovelling. Political fanaticism has blinded the worthy Doctor.

A church in his image 'would be a papacy worse than Rome'.

What had aroused the *Scotsman*'s ire was a passage in the address in which Chalmers digressed to warn the gathering of the dangers of civil unrest. It was their duty, he said, to guard against the lawless and revolutionary politics of those who spoke evil of dignitaries and were given to change. He meant Chartists, socialists, one-man-one-vote universal suffragists, trade-union rioters and the like – all who might have been tainted by the legacy of the French revolutionaries. The protesters were not to be accused of turning the world upside down. They were for peace, law and order, not for tumult, turbulence and confusion. (Here, there was great applause.) If left to go peacefully and quietly, they would soon prove themselves the best friends of social order, happiness and peace, and the aristocracy of the land would find it to be so. With men attempting to pull down the aristocracy, they had no sympathy. Free they were, but they were not anarchists. Beware the applause of the multitude, for 'still more galling than the tyranny of the state is the tyranny of the multitude'. No Tory could have expressed it more forcibly.

With this warning, Chalmers touched a nerve. Fitful memories of the Revolution still haunted the privileged classes, though it had happened fifty years before and in another country. And there had been more recent and closer symptoms of unrest, alarming enough to send a shiver down respectable spines. Not long since, handloom weavers in the west of Scotland and their allies had marched with weapons in their hands in the 'Radical War' of 1820, under the banner 'Liberty or Death'. Liberty, whatever that was, was not achieved, but some found death: the ringleaders were hanged on Glasgow Green or strung up in front of the Tolbooth at Stirling. Henry Cockburn, who drew up the Scottish Reform Bill that was passed in 1832, watched with mingled satisfaction and alarm a huge, though mercifully peaceful, workers' demonstration in the bill's favour pass through the centre of Glasgow. 'Gratifying but fearful', he said, dreading the consequences if the populace were to take the law into their own hands. Reform was a double-edged sword. A modest increase in the franchise suited Whigs like Lord Cockburn. Democracy was another matter. It stank of anarchy.

Hugh Miller, friend of the oppressed though he was, was no champion of democracy, and 'kept some of his deepest bile for political radicals like the Socialists and the Chartists', as George Rosie wrote in his *Hugh Miller: Outrage and Order*. Chalmers, Miller, Cockburn and those of their mind were scandalised by the Chartists' call for universal suffrage, secret ballots and annual parliaments — claims repeated in the second Chartist petition presented to Parliament in 1842. Universal suffrage 'in the present state of public morals' would ruin the country, said Miller — 'the masses are not fit for it'.

It didn't help that radicalism sometimes carried the taint of atheism. Not, however, in the case of Henry Vincent, a notable Chartist agitator — and lay preacher — who fought, and lost, of course, a by-election at Kilmarnock in 1844. It was probably then that he visited Rock House and had his portrait taken by Hill and Adamson. Vincent, who had recently spent a term in jail for his association with a miners' strike in Wales, is the picture of respectability in his dark suit and silk-sheened waistcoat.

In *The Cotter's Saturday Night*, Robert Burns had presented a soothing image of virtuous poverty which continued to be a comforting icon for the privileged and the propertied. But when Burns donned his Phrygian cap, it was a different story: he undercut this vision of domestic piety and subservience with disconcerting candour, as in his *The Tree of Liberty*, published posthumously in 1838 when it was safer to do so than in his lifetime. The Tree of Liberty was planted on the site of the Bastille.

> Upo' this tree there grows sic fruit …
> Gif ance the peasant taste a bit,
>   He's greater than a lord, man.

It was a disturbing thought.

While crowded Tanfield echoed to the cheers for Thomas Chalmers, it was altogether quieter in the tasteful but now half-empty oval of St Andrew's kirk, where the proceedings of the 'residuary assembly', as the *Witness* scornfully christened it, continued in some initial embarrassment. First there was a reshuffling on the benches. Here come the Forty Thieves! This was the group of evangelical-minded men who shrank from cutting the tie with the established church. 'We are forty', retorted one of them when taunted with belonging to a hopeless minority – and a nickname was coined. More politely, they were known as the middle party. Now they moved over from wherever they had been sitting to occupy opposition seats left vacant by the departed hundreds, 'rushing across the house to fill up the yawning gulph which the recent ecclesiastical earthquake had made in the forum of the church', as a partisan writer described it at the time, though, having left the church himself, he hadn't witnessed it.

They got no thanks for their soul-searching hesitancy. Viewed as deserters from the great cause, as a modern church historian says, they drew the scorn, derision and hatred of their former brethren on their heads; 'but the Church of Scotland would have been fortunate had there been more of them'. Such is the fate of middle parties.

Now Dr Cook rose to lament what had happened; but, 'darkened as the prospect may be, we do not despair'. They should all 'pray for the peace of our Jerusalem that all who love her may prosper'. Some ill-feeling was expressed over the credentials of seven ministers – the Strathbogie Seven, of whom more will be heard – who had been suspended from the ministry by a previous Assembly for putting the edict of an earthly court above holy writ. Some hissing broke out at the mention of their names, but, after soothing words, the meeting turned to the election of a Moderator for the coming year.

Dr Cook knew the very man: John Duncan Macfarlane, principal of Glasgow University and minister at Glasgow Cathedral. There was an objection; but the objection was overruled, and Macfarlane, who had been waiting in the wings already clad in his robes, entered and took the chair to mingled cheering and more hisses. His first duty was to call for the Queen's message to be read: 'Right reverend and well beloved, we greet you well …'. Victoria, or her advisers, hoped that Christian charity would prevail, and warned with 'more than usual earnestness and anxiety' against schism. There was a sting in the tail: she reminded them that, by law, ministers of religion were bound to obedience by their 'sacred calling'. Finally, 'We commend you to the guidance of divine providence, praying that you may be directed to the adoption of wise counsels'.

It was too late, of course. Schism had happened, and the schismatics had left the building. After a prayer for a spirit of meekness, forbearance and Christian love, a committee was set up to answer the Queen's letter and to congratulate her on the birth of the new princess, and a pastoral letter was called for to advise the people of Scotland to stand fast in the old paths. At six o'clock the Moderates dispersed, when it was observed that the galleries were almost empty.

Five days later, the Disruption was formally ratified at Tanfield. Almost 500 ministers came forward to sign the document resigning their right to stipend and manse. This was 'the signing of the Act of Separation and Deed of Demission', the scene captured by Hill and the title carved on the frame of his painting. They came forward in groups of ten, and the signing took several hours. Though Chalmers signed first, the man shown with the pen in his hand in the picture is Patrick MacFarlan of Greenock, chosen because he gave up the richest living of all − £1,000 a year, a great sum at the time. The size of his sacrifice earned him the starring role, but he was probably comfortably off in his own right, having a country estate in his possession. Others gave up less but suffered more.

It wasn't Hill's first choice as subject. A few of his early sketches survive, most of them giving only a suggestion − no more than stray hints − of his early intention: a few clusters of heads, studies of hands holding a Bible or document, a gesturing arm and pointing finger. The lines are faint but still clearly visible. Occasionally he has roughed in a group addressed by a standing figure. They may have been drawn on the spot, swiftly, just a few strokes of the pencil on a pocket notepad in the crowded Tanfield Hall.

A larger pen-and-wash drawing shows what was in his mind before he had his change of heart. A few principal figures cluster on a dais in the foreground with no more than a suggestion of the spectators massed around them. There's a liveliness, a freedom and zest in the drawing that the finished picture lacks. The centre of interest is Thomas Chalmers, gowned and with right arm raised and left hand clasping the desk before him;

obviously he's in full flight. The characters around him stand or sit in a variety of attitudes, some casual, some erect, all attentive. Documents are piled on a desk below the preacher. At the side, one man leans a nonchalant elbow on the back of a bench. Another, who seems to be wearing a plaid – there's a suggestion of tartan – crosses one leg over the other and rests an elbow on his knee. Could he be Hugh Miller? Impossible to tell; his face is turned away.

There's an intriguing detail. Among the books and scrolls littered on the floor, a young man in knee breeches lounges on the steps of the dais, his nose in a book or paper on his lap, reading. His arm rests on a box or chest which has an upturned top hat on it. Who he is or why he's there is a puzzle. The scene is lively and vivid – say, like a contemporary illustration for Dickens: D. O. Hill as Cruikshank or Phiz.

Sometime during the ten days of the Assembly, David Brewster came looking over Hill's shoulder and put him in touch with Adamson. Another who observed Hill there was Dr Robert Gordon, minister – or, rather, former minister, now that the die had been cast – at St Giles. Gordon had a key role in persuading Hill to think again. It was he who, demurring at the prominence which Hill planned for Chalmers in his vision, proposed 'something that would signify the completion of the Disruption'. So, in place of the orator, a stroke of the pen.

The momentous assembly ended on a devout but optimistic note with the singing of a psalm:

> Pray that Jerusalem may have
>   peace and felicity.
> Let them that love thee and thy truth
>   have still prosperity.

Hill recalled the parting moments of the Assembly with some emotion when he came to write his prospectus for the picture more than two decades later. His emotive words reflect the elegiac faith of a sixty-four-year-old, compared to the enthusiasm of a man of forty about to embark on a great adventure:

> Then cometh the blessing and dismissal – the lingering, long-drawn-out skailing of the Great Assembly, the tears at parting, the crossing of the willowy brook by its improvised rustic bridge, the earnest converse on the way home in the summer night … Farewell, dear Tanfield! Hallowed is thy memory for evermore!

In the same prospectus, Hill referred to a phenomenon that had been much talked about at the opening of the Assembly. The day had turned cloudy, casting the interior of Tanfield into such deep shade that it was difficult to distinguish the more distant faces in the gloom. But when 'nearly four thousand' voices broke into Psalm 43: 'O send thy light forth, and thy truth', the hall was suddenly 'filled with beaming light, from the bursting forth of the sun dispelling the darkness'. Coincidence, of course, as all agreed, not admitting to superstition; but it was comforting all the same. Hill borrowed the sunbeam for his picture.

When it was all over, an eminent Free Church man, recalling in later years the exaltation of the time, said that a spirit had been abroad, the same spirt that had 'hovered much about Bethlehem and Nazareth, Gethsemane and Calvary, the cross and the crown, the empty tomb and the crown of glory. It warmed our assemblies, it coloured our enterprises, it drew our hearts together, it sent us on our way rejoicing.'

The writer of a church history in the following decade gave a less exalted view of these events. 'Never perhaps in the history of any Church has so great a voluntary sacrifice been made for so slender a principle', he wrote. But he was a stalwart of the Auld Kirk that remained in possession of its gear. Or, as a perplexed farmer responded when told that the giving up of house, stipend and glebe was a matter of conscience: 'Conscience, conscience', he repeated – 'It's a puir conscience that'll no rax' (meaning stretch).

6

A message carved in stone

Hugh Miller set out for Sunday service in the Highlands at a church he did not know. The way was not well trodden.

> A path, nearly obscured by grass and weeds, leads from the main road to the parish church. It was with difficulty I could trace it, and there were none to direct me. The parish burying-ground, thickly sprinkled with graves and tombstones, surrounds the church. It is a quiet, solitary spot, of great beauty, lying beside the sea-shore; and as service had not yet commenced, I whiled away half an hour in sauntering among the stones, and deciphering the inscriptions.

Some stones were old, grey and shaggy with the mosses and lichens of centuries, and among them Miller found one ready for the chisel of an Old Mortality – the character in Sir Walter Scott's novel of the same name who travels the country rescuing the headstones of the Covenanting martyrs from decay.

'It lies beside the church-door', Miller recalled, 'and testifies, in an antique inscription, that it covers the remains of the "great.man.of.God.and.faithful.minister.of.Jesus.Christ" who had endured persecution for the truth in the dark days of Charles and his brother.' This man of God was the Covenanting minister Thomas Hogg, jailed on numerous occasions – once on the bare Bass Rock island in the Firth of Forth (where Stevenson had his David Balfour imprisoned in *Catriona*) – and finally exiled to the Netherlands for preaching illegally. On his return to Kiltearn parish after the Killing Time, 'fearing lest his people might be led to abuse the important privilege conferred upon them [he] gave charge on his death-bed to dig his grave in the threshold of the church, that they might regard him as a sentinel placed at the door'.

The inscription, still legible after a century and a half, closed with the warning that 'This.stone.shall.bear.witness. against.the.Parishioners.of.Kiltearn.if.they.bring.ane.ungodly. minister.in.here'. But in vain. The thing had happened, and the 'ungodly' man had entered the house in spite of the stone's silent witness.

Miller had heard that most of the parishioners of Kiltearn had deserted the place to worship in a neighbouring parish. On the way to Kiltearn, he had seen them as they passed by, the younger men the very picture of muscular Christianity, their 'rugged, robust form, half bone, half muscle – the springy firmness of the tread – the grave, manly countenance. There were grey-haired, patriarchal men among the groups, whose very air seemed impressed by a sense of the duties of that day.'

But they were going in another direction, and Miller was left on his own.

I entered the church. There were from eight to ten persons scattered over the pews below, and seven in the galleries above; and these composed the entire congregation. I wrapped myself up in my plaid, and sat down; and the service went on in the usual course; but it sounded in my ears like a miserable mockery. The precentor sung almost alone; and ere the clergyman had reached the middle of his discourse, which he read in an unimpassioned, monotonous tone, nearly one-half of his skeleton congregation had fallen asleep; and the drowsy, listless expression of the others showed that, for every good purpose, they might have been asleep too. And Sabbath after Sabbath has this unfortunate man gone the same tiresome round, and with exactly the same effects, for the last twenty-three years with a dreary vacancy and a few indifferent hearts inside his church, and the stone of the Covenanter at the door.

A gravestone played a prominent part in several portraits which Hill and Adamson took of Hugh Miller, who posed – postured, almost – for them in the cemetery on Calton Hill one sunny morning. He was a characterful model, a fine figure of a man; his description of the country church-goers could have applied to himself: 'robust form, half bone, half muscle, firmness of tread, grave, manly countenance' – this was the way he appeared in the calotype photographs which Hill and Adamson took of him.

In these pictures, he rests an arm on a carved headstone, in a clear reference to his former trade as a stonemason. In one, he wears a wide-brimmed hat, and one hand rests on a large mallet. One sleeve is rolled up beyond the elbow. Miller described this image in his article on the calotype in the *Witness* of July 1843, while concealing his own identity as sitter: 'a bonneted mechanic rests over his mallet on a tombstone – his one arm bared above his elbow; the other wrapped up in the well-indicated shirt folds, and resting on a piece of grotesque sculpture. There is a powerful sun; the somewhat rigid folds in the dress of coarse stuff are well marked; one half the face is in deep shade, the other in strong light; the churchyard wall throws a broad shadow behind, while in the foreground there is a gracefully chequered breadth of intermingled dark and light in the form of a mass of rank grass and foliage.' The stone still stands there, decorated with carved foliage and, aptly, a mason's dividers and square.

In another of the graveyard pictures – the better image of the two – he is hatless, the pose is more relaxed; the waistcoat unbuttoned as if he were resting from toil, both arms bare, one hand resting more naturally on the mallet, the other holding a chisel as the arm is crooked over the headstone. His magnificent mane of hair (unbonneted) is displayed to effect, and he has turned his gaze from the camera as if looking at an unseen point of interest beyond the frame.

Miller and Hill shared a commitment to the Free Kirk and were aware of their Covenanting inheritance. Both admired Sir Walter Scott's work; Hill contributed illustrations to an edition of the Waverley novels. The reference in these images to Old Mortality is clear – Miller drew the analogy himself.

A passage in *The Tale of Old Mortality* describes the plight of the persecuted Covenanting forefathers at the Killing Time. Scott had little sympathy with their extremism (or for the Presbyterianism of his own day), but he was moved by the tribulations of the hunted folk whom he called the Wanderers. He recalled that within living memory their stories were still current in the homes and hearts of poor country people.

> About forty or fifty years ago, melancholy tales of the strange escapes, hard encounters and cruel exactions of this period, were the usual subject of conversation at every cottage fireside; and the peasants, while they showed the caverns and the dens of the earth in which the Wanderers concealed themselves, recounted how many of them died in resisting with arms in their hands, how many others were executed by judicial forms, and how many were shot to death without even the last pretence of a trial.

The zealots who preached – outside the law – to their flocks who gathered in remote, secret locations were harried by Charles II's troopers. Some, like Richard Cameron, who gave his name to the Cameronian sect so vilified by Scott, were shot on the spot. Others were hauled away to be executed by the state. It was not just the leaders who paid the price: 'In general the sufferers were humble people, peasants, or mechanics of independent minds, who could not or would not clear themselves of suspicion of having some degree of sympathy with the Cameronian doctrines. In many cases they were butchered without a legal trial.' Evangelical Presbyterians of a later age seldom failed to identify with them.

Scott continues: 'A still sadder memorial of those calamitous days was the number of headstones and other simple monuments which were erected over the graves of the persons thus destroyed. These mortal resting-places of the victims of persecution were held so sacred, that about forty years since an aged man dedicated his life to travel through Scotland, for the purpose of repairing and clearing the tombs of the sufferers. He acquired the nickname of Old Mortality.' Scott regretted that folk memory had grown dim, and that 'this species of traditional history is much forgotten'. For lack of a new Mortality, the neglected monuments of the martyrs had again been overgrown by moss and weeds.

The amnesia was not total. The Kirk claimed descent in a direct line from the founding John Knox and then the Covenanting martyrs of a century later whose hallowed names continued to be invoked by preachers, at least those of the more Evangelical sort.

Painters, too, found a rich source of inspiration in the old traditions. Historical painting flourished in the early nineteenth century; and Scottish artists, with Sir David Wilkie in the lead, found a rich theme in the heroic saga of their Presbyterian past. Wilkie, by then resident in London and, according to one view, 'the most influential artist of his day, Turner and Constable not excepted', toured Scotland in 1817 with a copy of *Old Mortality* – just published and all the rage – in his bag. He visited the scenes it described, and stayed at Abbotsford as Scott's guest. He also talked with Thomas Chalmers – so he met both the wizard and the lion of the north.

George Harvey painted *The Covenanter's Preaching* in 1830. A small gathering of the faithful – men and women of all ages – huddle around their preacher in bleak moorland, their faces lit by a stray shaft of sunlight. As he speaks, the preacher thrusts forward his pocket Bible in a defiant gesture. Some of the men clutch guns along with their bibles; one sits on the ground with a sword at his side. There are dogs and horses – one horse with a solemn male rider, another with a woman perched side-saddle, riding pillion. The heather moor stretches towards a pale sunset, with the distant figure of a man silhouetted on top of a dark knoll, standing guard. If there's an attack, there'll be bloodshed. This lone preacher, these sheltering men, women and children, are in danger of their lives.

The point is affirmed in Thomas Duncan's painting, *The Death of John Brown of Priesthill*, dating from 1844, one year after the Disruption. Scott's words, taken from his note to an old narrative, describe the event. John Brown lived in an isolated cottage where the Covenanting prophet and preacher Alexander Peden, on the run from the dragoons, had taken refuge overnight. Early on a foggy morning two days later, Brown was surprised by horse soldiers led by Graham of Claverhouse, whose name was a byword for cruelty in the Killing Time – 'Bluidy Clavers' he was called, with justification. After a brusque interrogation in the presence of Brown's wife and family, Claverhouse gave summary justice: 'Go to your prayers, for you shall immediately die'.

Brown kissed his wife and family and was led out to face a firing party (the flash of their musket shots dazzled the poor woman). 'The most part of the bullets came upon his head, which scattered his brains upon the ground.' After a coarse jest at the widow, Clavers galloped off with his men. 'She set the bairns on the ground, and gathered his brains, and tied up his head, and straightened his body, and covered him in her plaid, and sat down, and wept over him.'

Scott, as so often, swithered between admiration for deeds of the past and support for the Tory orthodoxy of his day: 'While we read this dismal story we must remember Brown's situation was that of an avowed and determined rebel, liable as such to military execution.'

Duncan's picture belongs to the world of melodrama and high romance. In the foreground, the figure of the slain

Covenanter lies spreadeagled. The hair is wild, the forehead ghastly pale but apparently unmarked, no brains in sight. A blanket partly covers the body and stretched-out arms where he lies almost in crucifixion pose. Beside him, his distraught and comely widow, half in a faint, clasps her frightened infant at her knee with her stepdaughter at her side. The martyr's dog has shared his fate, stretched dead beside him. In the distance, the slaughtering dragoons ride off into the mists.

David Octavius Hill was a colleague and friend of both Duncan and Harvey. He knew Duncan intimately; they had been school fellows, and, when Duncan lay dying two years after the Disruption, Hill was at the bedside with his wife and family. He admired the work of both artists, but it was David Wilkie's that most inspired him. Wilkie had turned back to the Reformation and the founding of the Kirk for the subject of his *John Knox preaching at St Andrews* and his unfinished *Knox administering the Sacrament at Calder House.* He had barely roughed out the *Sacrament* before his death in 1841 – but still, it's a powerful image with Knox dominating, a head or two fleshed out and the rest tentatively sketched in. A year after Wilkie's death, with tension already growing over the threatened Disruption, Hill encouraged the Royal Scottish Academy to buy the unfinished painting when the contents of Wilkie's studio were sold.

He made notes on it, and it's conceivable that he used it as his model when he came to make his first sketches for the Disruption picture – a grand historical painting in its own way, but one that turned out to be very different from Wilkie's.

Once again, as Hugh Miller believed, God's servants in the Kirk were being forced to make a stand 'on the well-trodden battlefield of her saints and martyrs'.

The cause for which the Covenanters had risked their lives rested on their refusal to take an oath of allegiance to the king

(Charles II) which called on the Church to accept, among other things, the right of wealthy laymen – the so-called patrons and heritors – to impose their own choice of minister on a parish, regardless of the people's wishes: lairds' will against popular choice, privilege against the people.

In his poem *The Twa Dogs*, Burns had the mongrel Luath voice the sentiments of the common people on the subject:

> They'll talk o' patronage and priests
> Wi' kindling fury i' their breasts

– the church of Rome being the other pole of godlessness in the eyes of Evangelicals. Nearly two centuries after the Covenanters, the issue came alive again.

Ever since the Reformation, the right of a congregation to have the final say in the choice of their minister had been embodied in the constitution of the Kirk. It was implicit in Knox's *First Book of Discipline*, a cornerstone of the Scots Presbyterian faith, which laid down: 'it appertaineth to the people, and to every several congregation, to elect their minister'. Nothing could be plainer. An Act of 1690, following the Killing Time, abolished patronage and at the same time formally gave congregations the right to object to any candidate they found unacceptable. When patronage was reintroduced yet again at the time of Queen Anne, the right to object was not revoked. The 'call' – the acceptance of a candidate by the people in the pews – remained, at least in theory, an essential preliminary in the settlement of a parish minister, even if it was in abeyance throughout the heyday of the Moderates in the second half of the eighteenth century.

That began to change with the growth of an Evangelical movement – the 'wild party', as they were often known. The really 'wild' among them were democrats in politics as well as religion who wanted rid of patrons altogether. Others, like Chalmers, hoped merely to curb their power. 'Chalmers', as a historian of the Church put it, 'believed that a good use might be made of patronage to secure an effective ministry. He realized the danger of unbridled popular liberty of choice, for he was no democrat.' In the General Assembly of 1833 – just after the passing of the great parliamentary Reform Bill – when the Evangelical wing was on the eve of winning power for the first time, Chalmers proposed that if a majority of parishioners opposed a patron's choice, they should have the right to veto it. A patron, he railed, might be 'an infidel or an atheist, a fool or a knave, a scoundrel to society and a foe to godliness', and yet he had 'the chief power in the selection of the man who is to minister in holy things to a Christian congregation'. In spite of his eloquence, the motion failed by a hair's breadth.

The following year, when the Evangelicals finally gained the ascendancy, the vote was reversed and a 'veto act' was passed which declared that 'it is a fundamental law of this Church that no pastor shall be intruded on any congregation contrary to the will of the people'. Among those who opposed the veto was the dean of the Faculty of Advocates, John Hope, an Auld Kirk man who tabled his strong dissent and dedicated himself to destroying it.

The act was immediately tested. At Auchterarder, a small place midway between Stirling and Perth on the high road north, the death of the minister enabled the Earl of Kinnoull to put forward (or 'present') a candidate who, as required, preached in the church on two successive Sundays preceding his ordination. He didn't go down well. Only two parishioners signed his call, and 286 male heads of households (to whom the franchise was limited) turned him down flat.

John Hope seized his chance and took up his case, determined to have the Kirk's veto declared illegal. He took the case to the Court of Session, Scotland's supreme civil court, which deliberated at length before ruling against the Kirk. The Kirk's veto 'law' was no law and could not be upheld, and the spurned candidate was free to move into the manse, collect his stipend and preach with a clear conscience, no matter what his parishioners thought of him.

The Evangelicals were outraged. It didn't help that the second centenary of the signing of the National Covenant – the document from which the Covenanters took their name – was being celebrated that year. An appeal to the House of Lords was dismissed in the most humiliating way. Particularly galling were the contemptuous words of Lord Brougham, a former Lord Chancellor and an émigré Scot who had made an eminent career at the English bar and in Westminster politics.

Henry Brougham was an ambitious, capricious and immensely talented man. Charles Greville, courtier and civil servant to the Privy Council, closely observed 'this curious and versatile creature' and commented shrewdly in his diaries: 'After acting Jupiter one day in the House of Lords, he is ready to act Scapin anywhere else the next'. In other words, from delivering a solemn judgement on the bench, he could go and play jackanapes at a society ball. His conversation, according to Greville, was effortless and exhilarating: 'It is the spontaneous outpouring of one of the most fertile and restless of minds, easy, familiar, abundant and discursive'. Greville reports that, as a guest in the country at an aristocratic weekend, Brougham never stopped talking from the moment he arrived until he left, but without wearying his auditors:

> Brougham is certainly one of the most remarkable men I ever met; to say nothing of what he is in the world, his almost childish gaiety and animal spirits, his humour mixed with sarcasm, but not ill-natured, his wonderful information, and the facility with which he hands every subject, from the most grave and severe to the most trifling, displaying a mind full of varied and extensive information and a memory which has suffered nothing to escape it, I never saw any man whose conversation impressed me with such an idea of his superiority over all others.

As for the written word, he wrote 'with inconceivable rapidity, seldom corrects, and never reads over what he has written'.

Brougham could be equally electrifying on the platform and the bench. After opening a debate on the Irish question in which he spoke for three hours, his Tory opponent, the Duke of Wellington, declared it the finest speech he had ever heard in parliament. Probably the best cause to which he devoted his talents was the campaign to abolish slavery in British possessions, for which he delivered 'flaming speeches'. At the same time, Greville detected feet of clay, as when Brougham held forth in 'his usual daring, unscrupulous, reckless style, pouring forth a flood of eloquent falsehoods and misrepresentations'. Lord Cockburn was somewhat cool about his great contemporary. Brougham – 'ambitious to leave the marks of his footsteps everywhere' – had formulated a plan to introduce English counsel to the Scottish bar, a project to which Cockburn and his colleagues gave 'a decided negative'. Now, from his seat of power in the English establishment, Brougham put the disputatious Scots Kirk in its place. Or attempted to do so.

As the crisis deepened, Lord Cockburn noted: 'Scotland won't hear the last of this Auchterarder case for the next century'. Hugh Miller, entering the fray at this point, made sure that the issues raised at Auchterarder and in some later cases would resonate for at least the next decade, until the Disruption brought a kind of resolution.

Before Auchterarder, Miller had been occupied with other things. He had laid aside the mallet and the chisel for the white collar and a desk in a bank, he was eagerly pursuing his interest in geology, he had literary ambitions; he had a young wife and had suffered the agony of their child's death in infancy. Miller read through Brougham's speech with dismay. He was so distressed that he couldn't sleep: 'I tossed wakefully throughout a long night'. In the morning, he sat down and started to pen a letter addressed to Brougham but fully intended to reach the people at large. He spent a week at the task in his free time from the bank in Cromarty.

He began his *Letter from One of the Scotch People to the Right Hon. Lord Brougham and Vaux* with spare civility: 'My lord, I am a plain working man …'. (Plain! Miller, self-taught but shrewd and intelligent – too modest.) 'I am acquainted with no other language than the one in which I address your Lordship; and the very limited knowledge which I possess has been won slowly and painfully … I am a plain untaught man.' The opinions that Miller held on the law of patronage, he claimed, were 'those entertained by the great bulk of my countrymen' – too large a claim, as it happened, considering the great industrial underclass with no religion at all, and the substantial number of God-fearing common people who were content with the status quo. Still, there was considerable popular support for his views, as events were to prove.

He buttressed his argument by reference to the *First Book of Discipline* 'as drawn up by Knox and his brethren', which laid down that 'neither by the king himself, nor by any inferior person, should ministers be intruded on congregations, contrary to the will of the people'. (For the will of the people, read the will of the male householders in the parish, a somewhat diminished democracy.) He noted that, from the outset, the idea of patronage had been denounced in Presbyterian doctrine as 'an abuse flowing from the Pope and the corruption of the canon law', and contrary to the word of God. The right of patronage could be exercised 'by fools, debauchees, infidels'. He named none.

Patronage had 'rendered Christianity inefficient in well-nigh half her parishes' and had separated 'many of her better people from her clergymen'. Furthermore, he saw Brougham's judgement as part of 'a deep and dangerous conspiracy' against the liberties of his country. If the Kirk's stance had offended 'many of her noblest and wealthiest, and they are flying from her in crowds', so be it: 'let the chaff fly'. The Kirk would take up its position 'on the well-trodden battlefield of her saints and her martyrs'.

Having reached this stirring conclusion, Miller posted the missive, not to Brougham but to Robert Paul, the secretary and general manager of the Commercial Bank of Scotland, 'a gentleman from whom I had received much kindness when in Edinburgh'. Paul was an active churchman with an entrée to the circle of leading Evangelicals. He showed the letter to one of these, the up-and-coming young Robert Smith Candlish, minister of St George's Church in Edinburgh. Candlish at first laid it aside unread, but when he did look at it he rushed 'in a state of great excitement' to show it to others. All agreed: this was the propaganda they needed. It must be printed.

The tract sold out smartly: four editions each of 1,000 copies followed in rapid succession. It circulated widely and was read in high quarters. Lord Melbourne, the future prime minister, saw it and surmised that the pseudonym 'Hugh Miller' sheltered one or another of the Evangelical Scots divines; the Irish leader Daniel O'Connell admired its forthright language if not its content; William Gladstone, high Anglican and Tory (at that time) politician, cited it in one of his polemics on Church affairs.

The *Letter* was opportune. The idea of publishing a newspaper to reflect Evangelical opinion was in the air. Candlish and Robert Paul were involved; so were, among others, Alexander Dunlop, an Edinburgh advocate high in the counsels of the movement, and two churchmen soon to be eminent in the Free Kirk, Thomas Guthrie and William Cunningham. They had a newspaper in mind but no editor for it. It's said that, when Candlish read through the letter, he immediately cried: 'That's your editor!' The very man: a man of the people, intelligent, strong in the faith, a forceful writer and a hard worker – their 'sledge-hammer' to batter Moderates on the anvil. He was offered the job; and, after a pause of several weeks for reflection

– for it would interfere sadly with his geological and literary ambitions – Miller agreed.

Forty people contributed £25 each to make up the starting capital of £1,000. The 'practical printer' Robert Fairly not only undertook to see the paper off the press at his office in the old Horse Wynd but also contributed 'some hundreds' more, while John Johnstone of Hunter Square committed himself as publisher to a year's run. Thus Miller was installed as editor of the *Witness* broadsheet, to appear twice weekly, on Wednesdays and Saturdays, under a defiant motto taken from John Knox: 'the truth I speak, impugn it whoso list'; with an annual salary of £200 guaranteed. The first edition came out on 15 January 1840, with a hard-hitting editorial on the two parties in the Church which set the tone for what was to follow. No one could accuse it of impartiality; Miller made it ardently partisan in the Evangelical cause. This has to be borne in mind when the *Witness*, as so often, is the chief source of information about the developing controversy.

There was a lot of reading in it. In size, it was larger than today's broadsheets, carrying seven wide columns of tightly packed small print on each page, broken only by minimal headings. All type had to be set by hand, letter by letter. The only illustrations were small line-drawn vignettes – they might be a railway engine or a coasting vessel – among the small ads which filled the front page. During the Disruption Assembly, the print run was increased to three editions weekly, and sets of all nine papers containing the Assembly reports could be ordered in advance. It had been promised that 'at whatever period the expected disruption may take place, we shall be enabled to give full reports of the business of *both* assemblies' – and the pledge was triumphantly met. On 23 May 1843, it was announced that demand for these sets had far exceeded supply, and that 'upwards of 11,000' had been sold in one day.

Possibly many copies of the paper were distributed by mail order – some of the editions to be seen in Glasgow's Mitchell

Library are addressed on the front page to a Miss Stewart of Lewis Street, Stranraer. From an initial circulation of 600 copies, it soon rose to 1,800 and at its peak reached nearly 4,000. For a time, it outsold the *Scotsman*.

The driving force was always Miller, though how many assistants he had – part-time or otherwise – is hard to tell. One man could not hope to fill the columns, though his personal output was vast. Yet he is said to have been a slow and laborious writer, 'trying out every sentence on his ear'. The *Glasgow Herald* at roughly the same time had an editorial staff of two, the editor and a reporter, with a correspondent in Edinburgh and another in Paisley. A handful of subjects in the Hill and Adamson collection of calotypes at the Scottish National Portrait Gallery are listed as reporters or sub-editors on the *Witness*.

Possibly Miller's chief assistant in the early years was the Rev. James Mackenzie, co-author of a biography of the eminent theologian William Cunningham, who described Cunningham stepping up 'our dingy stair' to the printing office, where he would spend time preparing an article for the printer, or drinking coffee made 'in our gigantic coffee pot, Hugh Miller meanwhile toasting cheese' on a fire shovel. He looked back fondly on cheery times there.

Miller was justly proud of his contribution to the Evangelical cause. When attempts were made to curb his independence in the editor's chair, he could claim: 'I have been an honest journalist. During the seven years I have edited the *Witness*, I have never once given expression to an opinion which I did not conscientiously regard as sound, nor state a fact which, at the time at least, I did not believe to be true.'

Summing up his achievement, Donald Macleod, the current principal of the Free Church College, has written: 'No single influence told more mightily on the church controversy than the influence of Hugh Miller and the *Witness*. Perhaps it did more than the clerical mind was altogether prompt to admit.' For sixteen years, the *Witness* under Miller was to be the word of the Evangelical party, the living history of the movement and its conscience. The Moderates – even though most of the press was on their side – had nothing to touch it.

Though Miller never confined his columns solely to religious topics, Kirk politics and the Evangelical cause remained his staple fare in the *Witness*. Some years after the Auchterarder affair had been dragged through the courts, there arose what Miller and his colleagues saw as a new affront to the independence of the Kirk. He gave it chapter and verse. This time, his editorial ire was aroused by events in a small rural community in the north-east of Scotland, in an area traditionally of Moderate opinion. The place was called Marnoch.

7

Hey, Johnny Hope (a reel)

Now it seems laughable – the cartoonists thought so. But, for many, it was deadly serious.

In January 1841, when her copy of the *Witness* reached Stranraer, Miss Stewart learned that the weather in distant Banffshire had been atrocious. Severe storms had blocked all roads into the tiny village of Marnoch, where the snow lay more than two feet deep, and the swollen river Deveron gushed under a covering of ice. If anything, a thaw only made matters worse. Only the most determined people or the foolhardy ventured out of doors. Yet, bad as the conditions were, people struggled to get to Marnoch from far and wide – from nearby villages, from the towns of Keith and Huntly, even from places on the North Sea coast a good fifteen miles away. 'Early in the morning they were seen, in little companies, coming from every quarter, with some stout man leading the way, and oftimes an individual taking the duty of breaking a path in turn, and all his companions following in a line.' By ten o'clock, a considerable throng had gathered round the village manse, and still they came.

The events at Marnoch that wintry Thursday, 21 January, brought matters to a head in the increasingly bitter confrontation between Kirk and state. It was the latest in a series of disputes over the unpopular 'intrusion' of a pastor on an unwilling parish, and the most severe. After what happened there, the prospect of disruption in the national Kirk became a virtual certainty. Only a miracle could save it from schism; and the age of miracles was past.

The occasion was the formal induction of a new parish minister, one John Edwards, who had been presented in the name of the patron and was backed by a majority of seven ministers – all of them Moderates – in the presbytery of Strathbogie, in which the parish of Marnoch lay. Presbyteries are a grouping of parishes by area. They are one step up from the grass roots in Church government – but are subject, in turn, to the authority of the General Assembly of the Kirk, which can overrule their decisions.

Edwards was vehemently opposed by the four Evangelical ministers of Strathbogie presbytery, and by his intended parishioners, almost to a man. Who knows what Edwards had done, or not done, to arouse such animosity? Disliked he was. A schoolmaster in the neighbourhood for twenty years, with a licence to preach but no pulpit to preach in, Edwards had been for a spell assistant to the elderly minister, William Stronach. Shortly before his death, Stronach dismissed him.

The 'call' to Edwards, when it came, was derisory. Only one man signed it, a Peter Taylor, the local innkeeper. A total of 261 opposed him. Yet Edwards was persuaded to take the matter to law. It was a foolish move. What could he hope to gain? A manse and a meal ticket for life, of course, but on the other hand the certainty of contempt and humiliation from the people among whom he had to live and whose spiritual guide he was supposed to be.

Both the Court of Session and then the House of Lords on appeal ruled in his favour. The Kirk in Assembly refused to budge – Edwards would not do. It ordered the seven Moderate ministers – the 'Strathbogie Seven' – to heel. They must do as the Assembly bid and reject the innkeeper's man, even if it meant defying the law. The seven hesitated. But, when threatened by a lawsuit in which Edwards sued the whole presbytery, his sympathisers included, for failing to carry out the verdict of the courts, and sustained, furthermore, by legal advice from John Hope, they resumed support for Edwards and were promptly suspended from their ministry by the Kirk for insubordination.

To an outsider, this whirligig had a farcical air. A cartoon headed 'The Reel of Bogie', which caricatured the chief characters, showing Chalmers and the other main participants engaged in an undignified dance, toe-tapping and heel-kicking in their robes, was widely circulated and sniggered at, though how many recognised the sly ambiguity in the title is debatable. To 'dance the reel of Bogie', according to the Scots dictionary, is to have sex.

News from Marnoch on the fateful day came late to the outer world. The edition of the *Witness* which should have carried it regretted that high winds and rough seas had caused 'unusual delay' to communications with Aberdeen, particularly at the Tay and the Forth crossings. 'It is believed that the mails have been detained at the ferries owing to the boisterous state of the weather.' The rest of the country, for the most part, had to wait a further five days before the story could be told in full.

Meanwhile, the *Witness* could only speculate about what had happened. Its leader column pontificated in double-spaced type: seven men who were to meet 'presumably did meet', to perform an act 'of impiety and profanity'. In fact, only five of the seven had turned up. One was in London, the other unwell. 'An unhappy man, a wretched man' (meaning Edwards) had lent himself eagerly to 'this heinous sin'; had brazenly stood before the seven to answer for his godly zeal, his love of Jesus and his desire to save souls — unless, of course, that question had been omitted 'lest the tongue should cleave to the roof of the mouth'. The writer, presumably Hugh Miller, judged that whatever ceremony had been performed it was a mockery, illegitimate, and that Edwards was no minister of Christ.

The full account which appeared in the following edition of the *Witness*, borrowed 'slightly abridged' from a report in the sympathetic *Aberdeen Banner*, covered more than five columns of dense print and ran to almost 7,000 words. It told that when 'the principal actors in the day's calamity' had ploughed their way to the village in their carriages drawn by four horses each, they arrived to find the as yet untenanted manse locked. How to get in? After some uncomfortable moments as a hostile crowd gathered round, one of the party, a solicitor from Banff, took the initiative. With an unlawyerlike resort to force, he prised open a window and vaulted through – tumbled, more likely, for the sash crashed down with him. Having gained entry, lawyer Forbes opened the door from the inside to admit the rest.

With the hour for the service of induction approaching, they all issued out again and walked through the snow towards the church, Edwards among them in his robes. The church door was grudgingly unlocked for them, though they had to force an entry through the throng at the doorway who were all jostling to get in. Local people surged into the ground-floor pews while strangers from furth of the parish were assigned to the gallery. Soon the church was filled to overflowing, with hundreds more disappointed and left outside in the snow.

Then catastrophe threatened. 'Shortly after Mr Edwards and his friends had entered, it became apparent that one of the beams which supports the gallery was giving way; and the front of the first seat was pressed out by the dense mass of individuals leaning forward upon it.'

Consternation. A mad rush for the doors, a crush on the jam-packed staircase. At this, a gentleman called Mr Stronach, son of the late minister and a magistrate, mounted the pulpit steps and shouted for calm, which was gradually restored, though the crowd in the gallery was seen to be noticeably thinner than it had been. A few more tremors were felt during the morning, causing the occasional flutter of alarm and another movement towards the stairs.

Several lawyers were on hand to advise the five beleaguered ministers and their charge, including two advocates from

Edinburgh and 'one or two other professional men'. John Edwards stood facing them with John Inglis, one of the advocates, at his side. The suspended minister of Keith opened with a prayer from the pulpit, but no sooner had he finished than a Marnoch elder rose to challenge the proceedings. An ill-tempered exchange followed between the elder and his agent, the Aberdeen advocate John Duncan, and the suspended ministers and their representatives, niggling over each other's right to be there, frequently interrupted by the restive audience.

'For what purpose are you here and by whose authority do you come?' asked Duncan sternly, prompting a particularly loud outburst of cheering and a surge of excitement, 'in the midst of which a creaking of the beams, or the snapping of a stool, alarmed again various parties in the galleries, but this time the infection did not spread far, and any dread that might have been felt was soon over'. Finally, Duncan was permitted to read out a 700-word protest on behalf of the 'elders and people of Marnoch' and signed by more than 450 of them, 'against the intrusion of Mr Edwards'. In it, they repudiated and disowned the 'pretended' ordination of Edwards, they held any act by the suspended ministers to be null and void and their presence that day to be trespass, and they alleged that the only interest Edwards had in seeking the ministry was financial: 'Are we to be sacrificed merely that Mr Edwards may draw the stipend?' Therefore 'we must, and shall, united, leave the Church and seek ministrations elsewhere'. A premonition of the great Disruption to come?

They left. As the offended parishioners picked up their Bibles, rose from the pews and walked out, bystanders waiting outside in the cold rushed in to take their places. 'Old men, with their heads white as the snow that lay deep on their native hills', were seen to weep as they crossed the threshold. 'They left the church now given up to the spoilers, and like the Israelites of old, passed from the house of bondage.' The writer found a moral beauty in their act.

Indoors, the proceedings became disorderly. Hissing, shouting and stamping interrupted the suspended ministers as they tried to have the intimation of Edwards' admission read out at the church door by the church officer, in accordance with the rules. But the substitute church officer, 'a man of the name of William Monro' who had been brought in from a neighbouring parish, couldn't force his way to the door and had to read the intimation from the body of the church, which he did 'in a tolerably strong voice'. The *Witness* noted with satisfaction that no member of the parish, not even Peter Taylor, the innkeeper and sole signatory of the call, could be persuaded to act as beadle, bellman or precentor. In consequence, the complaisant Monro took on all three roles, even leading the singing of the psalms.

The exodus of the Israelites led them downhill to a hollow by the crossroads where they were addressed by advocate Duncan. George Troup, editor of the *Banner*, followed them there, but note-taking proved difficult in the open. Returning to the church, he found that events had taken a nasty turn and the place was in uproar. Pews and passages were filled, and protesters had occupied the pulpit. Below it, the ministers and their allies cowered as malcontents pelted them with snowballs, bits of bread and small coins. Troup himself attempted to quell the demonstrations – though at first taken for a spokesman of the ministers and given a hot reception – and at length some kind of order was restored.

Meanwhile, Stronach the magistrate, who had left some time previously, had been sent for and had ridden to the village with a posse at his back – a squad of policemen. He entered the church alone. The suspended minister for Huntly, by the name of Walker, rounded on him: 'We have been insulted, sir, in the discharge of our duty and we claim your protection'. Stronach said he would endeavour to give it.

Walker: 'Are there any policemen here?'
Stronach: 'There are.'

Walker: 'I insist that they be called in.'

Stronach: 'When I find their services required, I will call for them.'

He turned to the occupants of the pulpit and told them to go, and 'the pulpit was accordingly cleared as quietly as the crowd in the passage would permit'. Then Walker spotted Captain Anderson, the police officer, and called on him to quell the still murmuring audience so that the service could proceed with due solemnity. He was about to make further demands when his lawyer persuaded him to shut up, and the magistrate called on Anderson and his men to clear the passages, but 'in the gentlest manner'; they were not to strike or handle the people roughly except as a last resort. The passages were cleared, the people sat still in their places, and the service continued.

Monro, the pro tem. beadle and bellman from across the parish boundary, sang two verses from the twentieth psalm:

> Jehovah hear thee in the day
> when trouble he doth send;
> And let the name of Jacob's God
> thee from all ill defend …

The suspended minister for Keith, who had taken possession of the pulpit, said a brief prayer and then delivered a discourse. The *Witness* found it inadequate, without specifying why.

Now followed the prescribed litany of question and answer, according to procedure. Edwards pledged that he believed the Scriptures to be the word of God, that he subscribed to the Confession of Faith, that he disowned 'all Popish, arian, socinian and other heretical doctrines', and so on, through nine headings. He would save souls, forswear worldly designs and interests, and promised to be a faithful pastor of the parish. The *Witness*: 'Need we say that a deep shudder ran through the whole assembly at this exhibition?'

It was almost over. 'We never saw a minister ordained, and have no single parishioner, no human being in his charge, to bid him God-speed, and pray for his wellbeing. So it was with the pitiable Mr Edwards.' True, Mr Peterkin, a lawyer from Edinburgh, wished him much joy – 'a cautious clever gentleman, thinking of his long bill'; a Mr Robertson of the *Constitutional* newspaper shook hands with him warmly, Mr Adam of the *Herald* less so. Captain Anderson took his arm 'with an air that said this is my duty' and escorted him out, with a policeman on either side. And the people hissed.

As for Edwards: 'We never knew a presentee so wretched. If he was not punished that night, in the bitterness of his thoughts, and if he is not punished day by day, in the recollection of those policemen, those guards – those hisses, those fearful hisses, then we say he is a man without a heart to feel, or a soul to think'.

Edwards – 'nominally minister of Marnoch but really minister of Peter Taylor' – vanishes from the story. He died in 1848 at the age of fifty-seven, having enjoyed his incumbency at Marnoch for seven years during which, according to one record, his 'prudent and conciliatory manner' won him the esteem and affection of many parishioners, even some of those who had opposed him. It's unlikely that he filled his kirk.

As for the Strathbogie Seven, Henry, Lord Cockburn, wasted no pity on them. 'These men', he wrote in his journal, 'are absolutely certain of retaining their stipends, manses, glebes, and everything else except being recognised by the General Assembly as ministers' – for which, he was sure, they would be hailed as martyrs by all the enemies of the Kirk. Huh! You can almost hear the snort. 'Better-backed martyrs or more comfortable persecution have never been.'

Nine months later, there was almost a replay of the affair at Marnoch, only a few miles to the south at the village of

Culsalmond, in the heart of rural Aberdeenshire. Once again, the patron presented a candidate rejected by the parish. This man, a sixty-year-old called Middleton, had already deputised for the elderly incumbent, who had become too infirm to carry on.

Middleton stood accused – rightly or wrongly; it's always possible in such situations that malice or ill-will came into it – of a string of faults: neglect of family worship, indulging in 'secular pursuits' on the Lord's day, laxity in his clerical duties, and – probably the most heinous of all – cold and unspiritual preaching. At any rate, Middleton was not liked.

Again, the final act took place in wintry weather. 'Stately Benachie [the local hill] looked down' on the scene, mantled with snow, as 2,000 people braved driving showers of sleet and massed round the church. At last the Moderate ministers of the presbytery issued from the manse with their man, headed by the county sheriff and a squad of constables. When the church doors were opened, sheriff, constables, Middleton and all were borne in helplessly and scattered pell-mell among the crowd as it rushed in. The presiding minister finally got to the pulpit only to find the Bible had been forgotten; the captain of police handed up his own pocket testament.

Still the service could not begin; and, after an hour of 'inimitable dumb show and noise', the presbyters gave up and returned to the manse to conclude their business there. Troup of the *Aberdeen Banner* was again present on behalf of the Evangelical press. After vain attempts to witness the ceremony in the manse, from which he was barred, he was admitted to the empty room when all was over. He could see no Bible, he observed severely, only an abundance of legal documents scattered on the presbytery table.

'It is thickening', Henry Cockburn wrote in his journal with increasing dismay as the crisis developed. And later: 'Thicker still. The ecclesiastical war goes on.'

Cockburn – silver-haired, hawk-like, as he appears in Hill's picture – a shrewd commentator on the Scotland of his day, opposed the hard line taken by his colleagues in the Court of Session, following the agitation led by John Hope and others. Hope had declared that 'Parliament is the temporal head of the church' and that the Kirk was 'wholly a creature of the state'. That view was put even more bluntly by Lord Campbell in the House of Lords: the representatives of the Kirk were 'public functionaries appointed and paid by the state; and they must perform the duties which the law of the land imposes on them'. Hope, again: 'That our saviour is head of the Kirk of Scotland in any temporal or legislative or judicial sense is a position I can dignify by no other name than absurdity'. All this flew in the face of the Assembly's solemn assertion that its spiritual jurisdiction was derived from Jesus Christ as 'the sole head of the Church', a jurisdiction which they were ready to 'assert and at all hazards defend' as their fathers had done 'even to the death for Christ's kingdom and crown'. The confrontation could not have been harsher.

Cockburn conceded that Hope and company might have been right at first, 'but they soon got rabid'. He called Hope wily and devious, and described him in action: 'Our high-pressure Dean screams and gesticulates and perspires more in any forenoon than the whole Bar of England in a reign'. He reckoned that there was no feeling among them except that of pleasure at 'winging Wild-Churchmen'. In his opinion, the court was provoked by its law being defied, 'but a Court has no right to be provoked'.

As an heir of the Enlightenment, he had little sympathy with the wild men of the Kirk; but he supported the less radical Evangelicals and he greatly admired Thomas Chalmers, his long-time acquaintance. 'I think I see the Church nodding to its fall', he noted gloomily on the eve of the 1842 Assembly, the last before the Disruption. That Assembly passed a resolution which even Chalmers had by then reluctantly come to accept:

patronage had caused 'much injury to the cause of true religion in this Church and Kingdom' and 'ought to be abolished'. The Assembly went on to adopt the celebrated Claim of Right which accused the civil courts of contravening the Church's liberties. Rather than abandon these liberties, 'they will relinquish the privileges of establishment'. They would be free.

That autumn, a great gathering of Evangelical ministers and elders – by invitation only – was held behind closed doors in Glasgow, a private convocation at which the inevitable break was prepared for. Though the proceedings were private, it became known that Thomas Chalmers had roused his hearers to a high pitch of excitement and enthusiasm for the cause and, more prosaically, had propounded a scheme for funding the new Free Kirk to make it financially viable.

Public meetings were held in the large towns, and deputations were sent round the country to prepare people for the split. One envoy, addressing a meeting at Langholm in Dumfriesshire, got a nasty shock. Referring to the voice of Scottish members of parliament being overborne by the English majority, he said on the spur of the moment that 'such injustice was enough to justify Scotland in demanding the repeal of the Union'. To his surprise, 'the meeting rose as one man, waving hats and handkerchiefs and cheering again and again'. He took care not to mention repeal of the Union at any other meeting. His experience shows how the defiance of the Evangelicals against interference by Westminster touched a widespread, if latent, nationalism. Ministers and congregations were pressured to commit themselves to the cause; some arm-twisting went on. Money was raised. And in the west end of Edinburgh, in preparation for the time when doors would be shut against errant congregations, the first 'free' church was built.

This was 'the brick church' – the auld kirks were stone – on Lothian Road, where Robert Candlish was to preach. Free St George's, as it was to be known, was a plain square building with brick walls, wooden pillars and a felt roof, and the interior was lined with paper laid on canvas 'having all the appearance of oak wainscotting'. It was described as 'neat, though humble' with an 'extremely handsome' façade. The gift of a wealthy donor, it was put up in less than six weeks, just in time to accommodate some meetings of the Disruption Assembly. (It survived only twenty years, and the Caledonian Hotel now stands on the site.)

The die was cast.

8

The greatest living Scotchman

Chalmers was the man of the hour, the unquestioned leader of the movement which became the Free Kirk. He was one of the outstanding figures of the day, revered by his followers in Scotland and known and respected far beyond. Personally, he could be charming, perhaps a little eccentric. Henry Cockburn noticed the 'quaint, picturesque oddity of his look, figure, and manner; his taste for cumbrous jokes, and the merry twinkle of the eye'. Graver cares, he said, had not quenched the 'frolicsomeness' of his youth. The essayist John Brown, in his *Horae subsicivae*, wrestles to give a description of the great man in his older years, his 'broad leonine countenance, that beaming, liberal smile; or on the way out to his home, in his old-fashioned great-coat, with throat muffled up, his big walking-stick moving outwards in an arc … his broad, simple, childlike, in-turned feet; his short, hurried, impatient step; his erect royal air; his look of general good-will …'.

The word 'leonine' was often used to describe his appearance and character. Chalmers knew; he joked about it to his daughter Anne when she was small: 'Some people even go so far as to call your papa a lion', he said. 'Oh Papa,' she replied, 'that would be a great nonsense.' John Brown remarked on the curious look of abstraction that sometimes veiled his eye – 'not vacant, but asleep – innocent, mild and large; and his soul, its great inhabitant, not always at its window'. But when he was animated, 'how close to you was that vehement, burning soul! how it penetrated and overcame you!'

Hugh Miller found a poet in the man. Soon after he first met Chalmers, he spent the best part of a day with him and some others, including the local minister, on a small boat sailing around the Sutors, the cliffs near Miller's home town, Cromarty. The day was calm, with a heavy swell rolling in from the North Sea, lifting and dropping the boat and sending columns of surf spouting on the cliffy shore. 'His face wore an air of dreamy enjoyment' – Miller guessed he would have preferred to be contemplating the scene alone. Their craft disturbed a flock of gulls whirling over a shoal of saithe and Chalmers, following their flight, asked the Cromarty minister if he'd not like to be a seagull. As for himself, 'I would', he said. 'I think I could enjoy being a seagull.'

The following year, Miller, again on a boat, was approaching Burntisland in Fife, where Chalmers was to meet him. It was a perfect morning. A faint breeze ruffled the still waters of the firth, and the wavelets sparkled in the sunshine. A thin wraith of mist was lifting from the distant city of Edinburgh on the far shore. As the boat approached land, Miller noticed a solitary figure standing motionless on the rock jutting into the sea just below the town. Miller disembarked, was not met as expected, and walked round to the rock where he found that the standing figure – motionless still – was Chalmers, 'the same expression of dreamy enjoyment impressed on his features as I had witnessed on the little skiff'. Only a true poet, Miller thought, could be so captivated by the scene.

Yet he could be purposeful, strong-willed, energetic and single-minded to the point of obsession. Thomas Carlyle – over the top as usual – called attention to the striking duality of Chalmers' nature: he was 'a man capable of much soaking indolence, lazy brooding and do–nothingism, as the first stage of his life well indicated; a man thought to be timid almost to the verge of cowardice, yet capable of impetuous activity and blazing audacity, as his latter years showed'. All this, having met him only twice with a thirty-year interval between the occasions. Carlyle thought him a man 'essentially of little culture, of narrow sphere all his life'. This from Carlyle's *Reminiscences*, written when the sage of Chelsea was in his eighties and had been long absent from his native land, and Chalmers had been dead for nearly forty years.

Cockburn, too, held that he was not 'a man of what is called learning', compared to some of his eminent contemporaries, even in church circles, but that his was 'a studious mind fraught with general knowledge'. But he saw in him qualities that set him 'above every Scotch clergyman since the Reformation'. In that sphere he was equal, and in one sense superior, to John Knox. Cockburn thought him the better orator.

Sometime in 1834, Chalmers suffered a quite serious stroke. Cockburn, who had heard he was showing symptoms of 'a tendency to paralysis', describes visiting the sick man. Some church matter was under discussion, and two presbytery men were with him. His face was gaunt and his voice guttural. He had risen from his bed wearing a nightcap, wrinkled stockings, slippers and 'a grey duffle wrapper', but insisted he was quite well, though weak. Most of the time he sat by the fireside resting his brow on the back of his hands on the chimney-piece, but when he spoke 'he sat upright and became inspired'. Cockburn said he'd never heard him more eloquent.

Often he aspired to a wider audience. Ever since his twenties, Chalmers had travelled to London – sometimes by sea, the best way to go before the railways – and made an impression. His first visits were made to further his career as a writer on scientific subjects; as he recorded in his journal in 1808, 'My great object is to get introduced into some of the literary circles' – he was promoting his book on political economy. 'The great success I have met with in Scotland encourages me to hope.' He was not always pleased with the company he met. 'Dined with Mr Sheridan [the playwright and wit Richard Brinsley Sheridan] and his admirers. Dinner wretched. A most offensive vulgarity.'

Later excursions were made as lecturer and preacher – and on these occasions he was lionised. 'All the world wild about Dr Chalmers', the abolitionist William Wilberforce noted in his diary in 1817. Then: 'Off early with Canning, Huskisson and Lord Binning to the Scotch Church, London Wall, to hear Dr Chalmers. Vast crowds' – so great the press of people that Wilberforce had to clamber up a plank to get in by a window, where 'young ladies of distinction' were also hauled in. Canning, then a cabinet minister, was moved to tears more than once by Chalmers' discourse.

Ten years later, Chalmers spent half an hour with Coleridge in his home at Highgate and found him unintelligible. On the other hand, Anne, his daughter, was enraptured. 'It appeared to me the most intense half hour I ever spent in my life, owing to the beauty of his tones and language, while he poured forth a monologue' – on the Book of Revelation, among other things. 'I burst into tears when it stopped.'

He was twice in London in 1830, joining the Scottish delegation at the coronation of George IV in the autumn. In 1838, he gave a series of lectures which drew the cream of society. The Duke of Cambridge sat on a sofa at the front, nodding his head frequently in assent. 'Monstrous clever fellow', remarked the royal dunderhead. Five earls, a marquess, and several peers and bishops turned up to hear him. The future Liberal prime minister William Gladstone, then a young Tory in his twenties, and always a high churchman, attended all the lectures and read the printed text afterwords. He was overheard muttering 'wretched error', and took up his pen to fire off a riposte.

All agreed that Chalmers was a great orator, whether in the pulpit or on the platform. As a young lecturer, when he set up classes in opposition to the decrepit professor of mathematics at St Andrews, he siphoned off the old man's students and even attracted the public as well. Later, when professor of moral philosophy at St Andrews, where previously 'the object of young men seemed to be to evade the divinity lecture, now the difficulty was to get a good place to hear him'.

In 1822, the English essayist, William Hazlitt, heard him preach in Glasgow with 'prophetic fury'. Hazlitt looked around at the packed and enthusiastic congregation and saw 'a sea of eyes, a swarm of heads gaping for mysteries and staring for elucidation'. Cockburn, listening to a passionate speech of Chalmers' in an assembly debate, found it better than the theatre. 'How he burns', he wrote. 'I shed more tears than I have done since they were forced from me by the magnificence of Mrs Siddons.' When Chalmers was a minister in Fife, his Sunday sermons attracted people from far beyond the parish boundaries, from St Andrews and even Dundee – no easy journey before the Tay was bridged.

Cockburn's friend and colleague on the bench, Lord Jeffrey, thought of Cicero and Demosthenes when he heard him. An American, one Nathaniel H. Carter, described him in action, sawing the air like the player king in Hamlet: 'He throws himself forward as if he would pitch headlong out of the pulpit; he clenches his white pocket handkerchief firmly in his fist, and brings down his hand as if smiting something at his feet … the orator seems convulsed with the throes of thought and the grandeur of his periods, rolling out one after another in rapid succession'. It reminded Carter of a Highland burn 'which at one time rushes impetuously down its rugged bed and then glides away in a deep and silent current'.

For all his impassioned oratory, Chalmers was not an extempore speaker. He had tried and failed, and after that spoke from shorthand notes. A member of the audience at his London lectures described how for the most part he spoke while seated in a chair, with his notes on a small table. From time to time when the spirit moved him, he'd rise to his feet, clutching the notes in one hand and gesturing with the other

– the pose Hill caught in his preliminary sketches for the painting.

One more thing: he spoke with a broad Scots accent, more common among public speakers then than now. His eloquence came clothed in homespun, to the puzzlement of his southern hearers until their ears attuned to it. In those days, the sound of Burns was still to be heard on educated tongues, and the 'correct' English of their written word gives a false impression of their speech.

Chalmers was born in Anstruther – which he pronounced and often wrote in the demotic, 'Ainster' – a fishing village in the East Neuk of Fife, an attractive corner of the coast now much visited by tourists and holidaymakers. He was one of fourteen children, son of a merchant. Both parents were devout Presbyterians.

The boy seems to have been a bit harum-scarum. He was sent to the university in St Andrews at the age of twelve, but such an early start was not unusual in those days. He was ostensibly destined for the ministry without showing much vocation for it. He even flirted briefly with atheism. His preference and great aptitude was for chemistry, mathematics and geology. By the turn of the nineteenth century, he was taking classes in divinity at Edinburgh, after which he spent a couple of years as an assistant minister in the Borders. From 1803 to 1815, he was minister at Kilmany, a country parish in Fife near where the Tay bridge now makes its landfall. Unmarried sisters kept house for the bachelor pastor in his handsome Georgian manse. The first years at Kilmany were spent in leisurely pursuits: Saturday evenings devoted to preparing his sermon, Sundays in the performance of his churchly duties, the rest of the week as he willed.

Even then, he was exercised with the problem of poverty, though he was never a supporter of indiscriminate charity, as extracts from his diary in those years show. 'Refused a wandering beggar an alms. It is a good general rule … let the money you have thus withheld be given to the unquestionable want that exists in your parish or neighbourhood.' And: 'A beggar called to whom I gave one penny after much hesitation. I should not give so much in cases of uncertainty.'

Since pastoral care took up so little time, he proposed a parallel academic career and secured a post as assistant to the professor of mathematics at St Andrews. It didn't last. To his chagrin, he was sacked after a year. This did not deter him from applying for the professorship of mathematics at Edinburgh, for which – as he pointed out in a letter – his church work would be no hindrance, since 'after the satisfactory discharge of his parish duties, a minister may enjoy five days in the week of uninterrupted leisure, for the prosecution of any science in which his taste may dispose him to engage'. These glib words of a twenty-five-year-old came back to haunt him in maturity when his views had changed.

The turning point came in 1810 in his thirtieth year, when he experienced a conversion to a stricter faith. There's a sugges- tion that a love affair went wrong, though, if so, his son-in- law's discreet biography says nothing of it. At this time, too, he had been much affected by the deaths of his sister Barbara and before that of his brother, both of them consumptives.

Shortly before Barbara's death, he had been asked to write an article for the *Edinburgh Encyclopedia* by its editor, the scientist David Brewster, mentor of Hill and Adamson. He had chosen a mathematical subject but changed his mind and wrote to Brewster asking to write on Christianity instead. But the crucial factor in his conversion was a severe illness – said to be a disease of the liver – that struck him down in late 1809, confined him to his bedroom for four months, kept him out of the pulpit for more than six, and from his full pastoral work for a year. The deaths of his siblings weighed on his mind; he believed himself to be about to follow them into the grave, and, during his long convalescence, he pondered on eternity. He emerged from the sick-room a changed man, claimed by the evangel. Today he'd be born again. 'The superficial faith of former years could no longer satisfy him', his biographer wrote. 'It could not stand the scrutiny of the sick-room; it could not bear to be confronted with death.'

From then on, his fame as a preacher spread, and Glasgow town council – an unreformed oligarchy which had the city livings in its gift – sought him out as minister for the wealthy Tron parish. He went there, but the hollowness of a fashionable ministry irritated him. He was expected to appear at too many public functions and sit on too many committees; to deliberate, on one occasion, on 'whether oxhead soup or pork broth was fittest diet for a poorhouse'. He seethed. He saw dire poverty and irreligion among the city masses and was convinced that the answer to both could be found only in a zealous, practical ministry and the creation of a caring Christian community.

Burns, perhaps, provided him with a model, a building block, for such a community. Chalmers knew, and was influenced by, the much-quoted poem *The Cotter's Saturday Night* – this being Burns in reverential mode, not in his earthier radical or satirical vein. It is a hymn to the virtues of pious domesticity. At the time when Chalmers underwent his conversion to a deeper faith, *The Cotter's Saturday Night* had a significant effect on the way he came to order his daily life.

In the poem, Burns imagined the cottar back from toil, with wife and bairns gathered round the fireside for their evening worship.

> The chearfu' Supper done, wi' serious face,
>   They, round the ingle, form a circle wide;
> The sire turns o'er, wi' patriarchal grace,
>   The big ha'-Bible, ance his Father's pride.

The cottar's humble worship is a domestic pattern of the traditional form and phraseology of Presbyterian devotions.

There is a reading from the 'sacred page', the singing of a psalm in 'artless notes in simple guise', and a prayer spoken by 'the Saint, the Father and the Husband'. Only the sermon is wanting.

Chalmers, once he had turned Evangelical, was so moved by the cottar's example that he reintroduced family worship, until then neglected, into his own household. And memories of the cottar family's solemn faith, integrity and homely sense of worth may have been in mind when – as will shortly be described – he quit his comfortable ministry at the Tron for the newly formed parish of St John's among some of the most squalid, godless slums in the city. It was, according to the poet, 'from scenes like these' – that is, the cottar idyll – 'that Scotia's grandeur springs'. Chalmers agreed.

Appalling slums existed in Glasgow and Edinburgh. In both cities, the contrast between wealth and utter poverty was extreme, all the more striking because they were juxtaposed within tight boundaries. Years later, Robert Louis Stevenson would write: 'From their smoky beehives, ten stories high, the unwashed look down upon the open squares and gardens of the wealthy; and gay people sunning themselves along Princes Street'. In Glasgow, a tenth or more of Scotland's population was huddled into a space three miles square. It had grown explosively with the industrial revolution, from a population of less than 80,000 in 1801 to 280,000 forty years later. Edinburgh's population doubled between the beginning and middle of the century. In the poorest areas of Glasgow, the human count was 500 souls to the acre. In Edinburgh, the Royal Mile, once the residence of the well-to-do who had decamped to the New Town, had degenerated into a sink of filth and disease.

Some years after the Disruption, a Glasgow printer, Alexander Brown, writing anonymously as 'the Shadow', reported on the squalor he found on nightly excursions into the poor quarters of his home town: *Midnight Scenes and Social Photographs, being sketches of life in the streets, wynds and dens of the city.* ('Photographs' was metaphorical; his pictures were in prose.)

Brown's investigations led him into canyon-like closes in the neighbourhood of the Cross 'into which the kindly rays of the sun never penetrate', watered by stinking rivulets 'of the grossest impurities'. He visited shebeens, the squats of the homeless, thieves' kitchens, dens that served as casual brothels. He saw sickness – a case he considered to be cholera, and everywhere the mark of smallpox.

One night in the Saltmarket, he follows a guide through a maze-like 'low damp, earthy-smelling, subterranean sort of passage' to a room where several scantily dressed men and women are preparing to sleep on two or three beds on the floor. 'We glance at the wretched hovel. It is small, ill-lighted, and worse ventilated. A dirty farthing candle stuck into the neck of a bottle diffuses a melancholy light. In a corner is a window, near the roof, just enough to grudgingly illuminate a prison cell. In an obscure part of the abode is a large filthy pail, apparently the urinal common to the entire household ... With many apologies we quit this so-called "home".'

He finds an old couple – the woman's face deeply wrinkled, the man's hidden – covered in scraps of matting, lying on the floor of a room so small that their feet almost touch the fireplace. There's no furniture, only a jar for water and some dirty cloths, and the floor is littered with brick and stones and broken laths and plaster. In contrast, as the clock strikes ten and Argyle Street is noisy with the constant rumble of horse-drawn traffic, he finds himself in the midst of a surreal phantasmagoria; pubs are ablaze with gaslight and all the small shops open, yet 'it looks, notwithstanding, as if hell were let loose':

we hear the cries of apple-women, fish and other dealers. Here, again, the idiotical jeer and senseless laugh of drunkards, who now stand in groups, or stagger across the street in quest of their miserable homes. There, again, are heard the horrid oaths and imprecations of low prostitutes – carrying their loathsome figures about with offensive boldness – flushed with drink, and bloated with disease. Others of these sorry unfortunates may be seen haunting the 'close mouths', spectres of death, rather than objects of life – waiting with restless impatience for a poor victim. Under such horrid scenes the streets continue to groan, more or less, for many hours together.

The historian G. M. Young created a picture of the hellish situation in which urban slum-dwellers lived: 'The imagination can hardly apprehend the horror in which thousands of families were born, dragged out their ghastly lives, and died: the drinking water brown with faecal particles …' and so on. His words referred to London in the 1830s, but they could just as well apply to Glasgow or Edinburgh a decade later.

David Octavius Hill's friend, Dr George Bell who looks over Hill's shoulder in the picture, wrote graphically of his forays into the lodging houses of Edinburgh, where the dregs of the population found poor shelter for the night: 'They are crammed full of a motley crew of the destitute, squalid, obscene, blasphemous, vicious and often criminal of both sexes, young and old'. He published a pamphlet called *Day and Night in the Wynds of Edinburgh* to draw attention to the scandal. 'The black-hole at Calcutta, in which men were stifled, has been described, and the hold of a slaver has been described; but no description *has*, because none *can*, be given of the interior of a low Edinburgh lodging house.' He thought such scenes defied the engraving tool of Hogarth, the pen of Dickens or the tongue of Robert Guthrie, the Free Kirk minister who made it his mission to improve the lot of the city's paupers, and who wrote that 'I have come up the College Wynd with the idea that I might as well have gone to be a missionary among the Hindoos on the banks of the Ganges'.

Where are the illustrations of street life in the raw? Not in the works of Hill and his contemporaries, not to be found on the walls of the academy on the Mound. The urchins in James Edgar's *Dr Guthrie on a Mission of Mercy*, painted in 1862, are plump and rosy-cheeked and show no sign of pallor, hunger or disease. Yet, presumably, these were the children of the paupers, beggars and vagrants described by Bell as living 'hidden among the masses of rotten, rat-haunted buildings behind the Grassmarket, Cowgate, West Port, Canongate etc.'. Bell was reminded of Dante's *Inferno*. The documentary illustration of poverty and disease on the doorstep of bourgeois Edinburgh was not a saleable item, and artists must live.

Bell described how typhus spread through one lofty tenement in the High Street, from top to bottom: 'The messenger of death descended'. Cholera, ever lurking after the great outbreak of 1832, was always a danger, its link with poor sanitation still unrecognised. Fever swept through Edinburgh in the autumn of 1843, and, during the three years to 1848, thousands of fever-sufferers were admitted to the Royal Infirmary there from High Street, Canongate, the West Port and the neighbouring closes. How many more suffered and died unattended?

Alexander Brown, 'the Shadow', reflected sadly: 'We are sure that the Christian community of Glasgow are comparatively ignorant of the physical and moral destitution of their fellow creatures'. Chalmers, the one-time leisured pastor of a country flock, the writer of theological treatises such as *The Messiah's Duties Considered* and *The Efficacy of Prayer*, wasn't ignorant. He had seen, he knew – and he determined to act.

Chalmers was able to put his theories to the test when he resigned from his comfortable ministry at the Tron in order to oversee the new parish of St John's in Glasgow which had been created from those east-end slums where the Shadow later prowled. He persuaded the town council to withdraw poor relief and allow him to attempt to alleviate poverty according to his own radical plan. In this, he was abetted by the publisher William Collins (whose family firm is now subsumed in the HarperCollins conglomerate). In fact, it may have been Collins, a man of wealth and influence, young though he was, who persuaded Glasgow town council to give Chalmers his head. Though only twenty-five, Collins was already an elder at the Tron when Chalmers arrived there, and Collins continued to work as his disciple, moving with him to St John's as his right-hand man in his great social and moral experiment.

Collins had impeccable Evangelical credentials. He was one of the early anti-slavery campaigners; tracts on the subject were displayed prominently in his shop, to the annoyance of some of his affluent customers, merchants who traded with the slave-holding West Indies. He corresponded with Wilberforce. He became an equally enthusiastic temperance man; drink was the devil. And, as publisher, he faithfully brought out Chalmers' voluminous works. The writer of a biographical sketch describes how Collins, 'quiet and unobtrusive', followed Chalmers 'with keen untiring activity, and soul on fire, testing the ideas of his chief, and giving them practical realization in the hovels of the poor, in the haunts of the godless, and in the dens of the profligate'.

In St John's, Chalmers established Sunday schools and day schools. The schooling wasn't free, a modest payment being demanded. There was never a free lunch in Chalmers' scheme of things. The aim, as the artist Thomas Duncan saw it, was to provide education 'so cheap that the poor may pay but so good that the rich may receive'. Chalmers divided the population of the parish – everyone, believers or not, apart from adherents to other churches like Catholics and dissenters – into clusters of about 100 households, each one assigned to the care of an elder who had to make regular visits to help, comfort, pray and offer spiritual counsel and support. Deacons were appointed to handle poor relief, for which they had to quiz the applicant closely to check that a dole was justified.

Charity, if that's what it was, had to be the last resort, since Chalmers expected relatives, friends and neighbours to rally to the aid of the distressed. Only when that failed would the church provide; and, since it was part of the deal in St John's that the kirk would assume responsibility for raising and distributing funds, these had to be met by church-door collections and the generosity of the wealthier members of the congregation. Chalmers had, according to Thomas Duncan, 'an admiration for that state of society in which a generous aristocracy shower blessings on the poor and the poor look up with gratitude to the aristocracy'.

It seemed to work, up to a point – though, in the end, Collins admitted to failure when faced with the intractable problem of 'drunkenness and immorality'. But satisfactory statistics were produced – for example, in one year the total cost of parish assistance fell from £1,400 to a mere £280, implying that the scheme was not merely charitable but cost-effective. Money could be saved as well as souls. On the other hand, how many poor folk simply opted out, tired of waiting for help, resentful of being interrogated by their betters or put off their religiosity? Whom could they turn to then?

Underlying it all was Chalmers' vision of the city as a grand collective of communities such as the parishes he had known at Anstruther or Kilmany. But Glasgow slums could never be rural Anstruther writ large. Small towns and villages had static or at least stable populations. Glasgow, swollen by immigration from the surrounding countryside, the Highlands and from across the Irish Sea, housed in its mean streets a seething, shifting, shiftless mass of the destitute and diseased. Even the better-off working classes, ever subject to economic vagaries, boom and bust, lived on the edge of the abyss of destitution. The problem could not be entirely solved, at least by the means Chalmers dreamed of.

In the years leading up to the Disruption, Chalmers threw himself into the work of church extension – the building of churches in the overcrowded and ever-growing quarters of the city, or in far corners of the Highlands where no church existed. Appalled by the irreligion of the slums and the poor working-class areas, Chalmers felt it was his mission to bring the gospel to the masses.

Mission, at home or abroad, was a keystone of the Evangelical creed. Chalmers spoke of the 'home heathens'. Abroad was infidel. An Edinburgh minister had called at the turn of the century for a mission to India to convert 'the natives of that distant, uncivilized, and benighted region, where our countrymen have flocked to gain riches, but have rarely sought to confer the far greater benefits of knowledge and true religion'. The call was heeded.

Above all, it was the matter of the Jews, the chosen people of old, now lapsed, that touched a chord. Had not Jesus enjoined the apostles to bear witness 'in Jerusalem, and in all Judaea, and in Samaria [a region of Palestine], and unto the uttermost part of the earth'? In this spirit the Kirk, in the spring of 1839, despatched a mission to the Holy Land (Palestine in common parlance), the Zion of Evangelicals ever eager to convert the Jews.

Four men set off on this adventure. The weightiest in all senses was Alexander Black, professor of theology at Marischal College, Aberdeen, who can be seen in the picture seated before a large atlas open at a map of Palestine – a portly figure dressed in a voluminous ankle-length topcoat. Presumably he discarded it in the Levant, where he suffered cruelly from the heat. It was considered that Black's knowledge of Hebrew would prove useful. With him were Alexander Keith of St Cyrus and two younger enthusiasts, Andrew Bonar, a minister from Glasgow, and Murray McCheyne of Dundee. McCheyne was an ideal choice. Still in his twenties, an acolyte of Chalmers who had recently been appointed to one of the new extension churches, he was one of the brightest prospects in the Church. He spoke of Jerusalem and Palestine with reverence and awe. His feet would tread the Promised Land.

The party crossed the Channel and travelled south through France. 'Poor Paris knows no Sabbath', McCheyne observed.

Rumbling through the countryside in their diligence, or stagecoach, Black amused his companions with the zeal with which he flung tracts from the window, shouting at the peasants in the fields: 'Voilà, un petit livre pour votre enfant' – a booklet for your child. They took ship at Marseilles and sailed via Italy to Alexandria, journeying onwards by donkey and latterly camel. Professor Black tumbled off his beast, but shook himself, remounted the camel and carried on manfully. In the rock-strewn desert on the approach to Jerusalem, McCheyne couldn't contain his excitement. He dismounted from his camel and ran ahead to get first sight of the holy city.

At Jerusalem, the professor was finally overcome by the heat and decided to return. He and Keith made their way home by the shortest route, following the Danube, while Bonar and McCheyne continued into Syria. McCheyne took to his bed in Beirut with a raging fever, and there were fears that it would finish him; but after a while he was able to continue by steamer to Cyprus, where he rallied. He and Bonar continued through eastern Europe, visiting Jewish communities on the way.

There was one further incident, described by McCheyne in one of his lively letters home. Outside a Galician village, he was menaced by two 'evil-looking' shepherds. McCheyne faced up to them holding his stout staff at the ready; but, finding he hadn't the heart to strike, he closed and grappled with them. They wrestled him to the ground but then, to his surprise, left him none the worse except that his coat was torn from top to bottom.

Meanwhile, Keith had fallen ill in Budapest: sickness was an ever-present hazard for Victorian travellers. He was nursed back to health by a Hungarian princess, a Protestant lady – as a result of which the first of the Free Church missions to the Jews came to be set up in Budapest rather than Jerusalem.

Bonar and McCheyne arrived home in November. McCheyne busied himself energetically in his pastoral duties in

the manner approved by his mentor Thomas Chalmers. These
included visiting the sick; he was careless, or unlucky, and he
caught typhus. He was not quite thirty when he died on the
eve of the Disruption, in which he had been expected to take
a leading role. McCheyne became the nearest thing to a saint
that Presbyterians could allow.

Chalmers, having proved to his own satisfaction that his
approach worked in St John's, stayed there for less than four
years before leaving for academia on his appointment as
professor of moral philosophy at St Andrews University. It was
back to bonny Fife and the seat of learning. Might this be seen
as a defection – the luminary abandoning his toil in the back
streets for the easeful occupancy of a college chair?

From then on, no longer a parish minister, he pursued a career
in the higher learning. After St Andrews, he became professor of
divinity at Edinburgh University, a post he held until forced out
at the Disruption. He declined all offers of a pulpit – several in
Edinburgh, and at the West Church in Greenock. The patron's
choice for that wealthy Greenock parish then fell on Patrick
MacFarlan, who, quill in hand, would later take pride of place
in Hill's picture.

Henry Cockburn's view of Chalmers was uncompromising.
For him, Chalmers stood out above all his contemporaries,
churchmen or laymen alike. To the judge, Chalmers was simply
'the greatest of living Scotchmen'.

9

Garden sittings by appointment

On the morning of Wednesday, 24 May 1843, the day after the signing of the Deed of Demission, the following paragraph appeared on the front page of Hugh Miller's *Witness*:

It is respectfully intimated, that arrangements have been completed for the Production and Publication, at as early a period as it can be properly effected, of

AN ENGRAVING

representing

The first general assembly of the Free Presbyterian Church of Scotland

From a Picture to be painted by D. O. Hill, Esq., RSA.

The Picture, the execution of which is expected will occupy the greater portion of two or three years, is intended to supply an authentic commemoration of the great event in the history of the Church.

Notice that it's not only advance news of a picture, but also an advert for the sale to the public, in possibly three years' time, of engravings to be made from it. It was a commercial pitch, and slightly premature, you might think, since Hill had yet to apply his first brushstroke to the canvas.

Hill hoped to win prestige and acclaim for his work, and no doubt a handsome fee from a prospective buyer (did he have a customer in mind – the Free Kirk perhaps?), but there was also money to be made from the sale of prints. These engravings were to be a generous size, the largest four feet wide, suitable for display on parlour walls, and selling at up to twelve guineas depending on size and the quality of the print ordered. The sale would benefit both the artist and his businessman brother Alexander, publisher to the Royal Scottish Academy, 'to whom orders for the Engraving may be addressed' at 67 Princes Street.

Memorabilia of the great event were already in demand, as indicated by another paragraph in a later edition which advertised the sale of copies of the Act of Separation and Deed of Demission, bearing facsimiles of all the signatures 'in sheets, rolled or stitched', mounted on calico at 1s 6d, or in cloth with leather case at six guineas.

So far, the breakaway church hadn't fixed on a name for itself. Free Presbyterian Church of Scotland doesn't trip off the tongue. A snappier title must be found. Also, the particular subject is unspecified, suggesting that Hill had not yet made up his mind. A 'great event' in the history of the church is rather vague. 'It will represent the Assembly at one of the most interesting points of its proceedings and will contain Portraits, from actual sittings, as far as these can be obtained' is as close as it gets.

Apparently, Hill had not yet fixed on the signing of the deed as the event to be recorded, nor on the form his portrait sittings would take. Though the meeting with Adamson had taken place by then, he may not have been certain that photography held the key. He was, at least, unwilling to commit himself publicly to it. Nor had he settled on the calotype process as the only method available to him, as an article by Hugh Miller in the *Witness* of 24 June reveals:

Mr Hill has been led by what at first seemed a scarce surmountable obstacle in his way, to have recourse to an expedient which bids fair to exercise no slight influence on his art; and to add greatly to the interest of his picture. Much of the value of a piece such as he contemplates must of course consist in the faithfulness of the portraits. There was an utter lack of time to get these taken in the ordinary way – and in a very few days, the members of the Free Assembly would have been scattered all over the kingdom … in the emergency the artist bethought him of having recourse for his likenesses to the recent invention of drawing by the agency of light. They were first taken by the Daguerreotype in the ordinary way, and with the usual sombre and shadowy effect, and latterly through the medium of the sister invention, the calotype – an art introduced into Edinburgh, during the last fortnight, for the first time, by Mr Adamson of St Andrews.

So maybe Adamson wasn't the only cameraman involved. And maybe, contrary to the evidence given by Brewster, he had been flirting with the idea of photography as an aid before Adamson and he had been introduced to each other. Other photographers were already at work in Edinburgh.

Furthermore, Hill had already decided to extend his cast list beyond those present on the chosen day – or, perhaps, at any of the sittings of the Assembly that May. The advertisement goes on to announce that not only 'the most venerable fathers, and others of the more eminent and distinguished ministers and elders' will be pictured, but that, among others, representatives of various dissenters 'who sympathise with, and approve of, the present movement of the Church', will be included, plus 'other personages who have taken, or may yet take part in the eventful proceedings of the Assembly'. So, in the space of a month, his vision of what the picture would include had already widened.

Finally, and fatefully, the timescale set by Hill was wildly optimistic – two or three years indeed! He had not yet appreciated the scale of the work he had embarked on and the labour that would be involved. Had he known, he might have paused – might even abandoned the project in dismay. But, for the moment, he is happily unaware that his grand painting will be as much a millstone as a masterpiece.

While the Assembly met, churchmen must have taken leave to sit in the garden at Rock House posing for their portraits. How many? Was there a trickle of them or a flood? It's not possible to say. There was an obvious attraction for them, apart from the novelty of having their photographs taken. A new experience! Curiosity, and a little vanity, may have entered into it; also a sneaky pleasure at having escaped for a little from the tedium of long-winded debate down at stuffy Tanfield. How pleasant to sit in the sunshine for a spell in shy Mr Adamson's garden, while his genial partner Mr Hill made sure that all was in order, setting you at ease, suggesting a pose, a tilt of the head or glance of the eye, a set of the shoulders or a turn of the face.

For Hill, these photo sessions, which he may have begun to employ simply as a useful aid to his sketching, soon became obsessional. Since the two-week period of the Assembly was patently inadequate for his purpose, arrangements were made to continue the work, sometimes at other locations. The next Free Kirk assembly, a special meeting held some months later and unusually in Glasgow, gave further opportunity for a burst of photographic activity, as did future assemblies in Edinburgh. But the work also went on outside these events.

Just days after the Disruption Assembly had dispersed, Sir David Brewster wrote to his friend Henry Fox Talbot that his protégé, Adamson, was now established in Edinburgh 'with crowds every day at his Studio'. Not all of these visitors would be Disruption figures, but many were. At the same time, Hill was sending lithographed letters to intended sitters suggesting appointments at Rock House. On 9 June, for example, Dr Robert Gordon, formerly minister of the High Kirk of Edinburgh, was invited to sit for his portrait 'with a view to its being made use of in Mr Hill's projected picture of the *First General Assembly of the Free Protesting Church of Scotland*' (another awkward stab at titling the new Kirk). Hill requested that Gordon 'will consent to meet him at Mr Adamson's house on Saturday between the hours of 10am and 2pm or on the Monday, Tuesday, or Wednesday following at the same time'. He added that the sitter would be detained only a very short time, 'the whole process being effected in a few minutes'. And if none of these suggested dates and times were convenient, the sitting could be arranged to suit Dr Gordon's convenience.

An appointment was duly fixed. The calotype was successfully made, and we have it today. In Hill's finished painting, Gordon is seen looking thoughtful with head inclined, one hand folded over the other, a perfect copy of the calotype image made at Rock House, except that between print and painting his hair has turned white. (Gordon died ten years after the Disruption, and thirteen years before the picture was finished.) Hill chose to age him in paint, as he did with a few others. Altogether, Hill and Adamson took about 1,000 calotype portraits in connection with the Disruption picture over a period of three years – by which time Hill's confident estimate of its completion date had been blown to smithereens.

While working on their Disruption portraits, the partners occasionally escaped to the seaside – to the fishing village of Newhaven, situated on the Forth a little more than a mile from the centre of Edinburgh. There, Adamson set up his camera out of doors to record the daily life of its inhabitants. In all, Hill and Adamson took more than 100 calotype images of the fisherfolk who lived and worked there, enabling them in 1844 to advertise a forthcoming collection to be titled *Fishermen and Women of the Firth of Forth*. It is a remarkable production, not merely in artistic achievement but also as a social record. Indeed, Sara Stevenson believes that the tight-knit little

Newhaven community, as portrayed in these calotype images, is an affirmation by Hill of the ideals which motivated Chalmers in his work in the Glasgow slums.

Life was not easy for the fisherfolk – for the men who were often at sea for lengthy periods as they followed the shoals, or for the women who gutted and cleaned the catches and carried heavy creels of fish for sale through the streets of Edinburgh. There's a fine portrait of a reticent beauty with her head framed in her shawl and her creel held in work-hardened hands. Hill captioned this picture variously as 'a Newhaven beauty' and 'It's no fish ye're buying, it's men's lives', echoing a line in the ballad *Caller Herrin* – 'Wives and mithers, maist despairin', ca' them lives o' men'.

Hard as conditions were, the tightly knit community held together through bad times and good, proudly independent – as the Hill and Adamson photographs seem to indicate. There's a heroic flamboyance in men posing on the quayside or by their boats, in their coarse canvas trousers the colour of sailcloth, their fringed neckerchiefs and their bizarre assortment of headgear. Sandy Linton (Linton is a fisher name) strikes a proudly defiant attitude, jaw set, face partly shaded by the broad brim of his hat, beside the bow of his boat, while his barefoot bairns squat under it.

Though the trips to Newhaven were undertaken as a diversion from the Disruption project, Hill found a way of expressing his admiration for the fisherfolk of the Forth when eventually he added the finishing touches to his masterwork. In the painting, among the onlookers peering down from the skylights in Tanfield Hall, is a figure in battered hat, with necktie awry. This is Willie Liston, Newhaven fisherman, instantly recognisable from the photograph that Hill and Adamson took on one of their outings to the Forth.

In 1861, Hill painted Rock House and its surroundings, showing a camera set up on its tripod but no sitter in front of it, and no Adamson behind it. It's called *In Memoriam: the Calton* – the Calton cemetery is visible in the middle distance. At first glance, the painting may seem to be a remembrance of his partner. But it's otherwise. The painting memorialises his daughter Chatty, who had died that year. Thus, at not quite sixty, he had lost his wife, Ann, an infant child, and now his adult daughter. His family were all gone. But there was a beginning as well as an end. In the following year, he married Amelia Paton, also an artist, and sister of his great friend, the painter Joseph Noel Paton. Amelia was to spur him on to finish the ever-waiting-to-be-completed Disruption picture.

There seems to be no detailed description of a Rock House photo session. James Good Tunney, who would become a photographer himself, spied on Adamson at work:

> Time after time have I gone and stood on the projecting rock below Playfair's monument on the Calton Hill, and drawn inspiration from viewing Mr Adamson placing a large square box upon a stand, covering his head with a focussing-cloth, introducing the slide, counting the seconds by his watch, putting the cap on the lens, and retiring to what we now know to be the dark room. Oh! if only I could have got an introduction to these men, it would have been the consummation of my happiness!

In due course, Tunney would get to know Hill, but too late, probably, for Adamson.

The elderly watercolourist John Harden, writing to his daughter towards the end of 1843, makes a brief reference to an appearance before Adamson's camera: 'I sat three various attitudes and three portraits taken'. His standing attitude, he says, was arranged by Sir William Allan (not Hill in this case), Allan at that time being president of the Royal Scottish Academy. The calotype shows Harden standing rather stiffly with one hand on hip and a sheaf of papers in the other hand. Allan adopted the same pose when he had his photograph taken, probably the same day. Another print of Harden shows him seated, a bald-headed old man with his lips parted (he looks as if he's lost his teeth), with an arm resting on two large leather-bound books on a table.

Books make a regular appearance in the calotype portraits. You can imagine them being carried out from Rock House along with all the furniture and other props and paraphernalia that the photographers required. Some books can be identified, like *The Land of Burns*, the album of engravings made from scenes that Hill had painted in the previous decade. Sometimes, a minister holds what purports to be his parish records – like Hugh Mackay Mackenzie with his *Free Church Tongue*, or James Julius Wood with *Malta 1843*.

The Holy Bible makes a regular appearance, of course, but not just to indicate the piety of the sitter. Books served as practical hand- or arm-rests while the subject held his pose for the required number of minutes. Elbows could be propped on a pile of books or a table. Hands on chin, cheek or brow steadied the head. A friendly arm on the shoulder gave mutual support. The skill was to make it all look natural.

But, often, mechanical means of support had to be introduced, with brace or bracket used to clamp a head or hand in position. Chalmers declaims with a brace supporting his outstretched arm. Ironmongery galore steadies two standing figures in a group portrait – a necessary precaution, since in a large group one or more is sure to move, jerk or twitch, resulting in a blur. In such cases, Hill painted or pencilled out the intrusive supports, either on the negative or when it was printed.

Hill and Adamson took a number of these group portraits, described in the catalogue – in the case of ministers – as presbytery groups. It must have been time-consuming, with Adamson preparing the camera and Hill shepherding his characters into position, chaffing, cajoling, giving them their 'parts', distributing the props, adjusting the supports, making sure all was well, and finally waiting nervously while they froze and the seconds ticked by. On the other hand, it was economical: Hill got eight or so likenesses in one shot instead of one at a time.

The more you scan these calotypes, the more familiar the background and the furnishings and bits and pieces become. They get to be old friends. A chair, for example, the one with the wooden arms that curl round to the seat like commas, turns up again and again. Many a Presbyterian posterior has settled on it. Another chair dragged out from Rock House to serve in the photo sessions is fancier, more ornate. From hints that you find in different calotypes – a corner, a leg, a portion of the back – the whole chair begins to take shape. The seat is plain and flat, the back is tall and elaborately carved, the legs turned in a corkscrew. Not a comfy chair, not restful, as the attitude of some sitters suggests. Sometimes, a small table with vaguely Egyptian or Assyrian features puts in an appearance. Household items turn up from time to time – a tall wineglass which can double as a vase when required. A bird in a cage, sometimes. Objects relevant to the particular sitter may be introduced, like the pair of dividers on the table beside Hill's friend, the engineer James Nasmyth. There is a ubiquitous brocade drapery with a fern or plant design which is quite a favourite – draped, swagged, drawn, folded – and a dark sheet or blanket that's often spread out behind to cut out clutter and make a plain background.

In many of the shots, a trellis, or a section of it, appears – possibly it's a porch framing the doorway. It may be partly masked by drapery or hidden by a standing figure, but a telltale glimpse of criss-cross slats gives it away. Paving stones can sometimes be made out at the bottom. This is Hill and Adamson's favourite spot at Rock House – here where the sun beats down, the tables and chairs are set in place, the books disposed, the sitters gather.

Unfamiliar features suggest a different location. Hill and Adamson followed their ministers and elders to Glasgow for a special meeting of the Free Kirk's assembly in September 1843, and set up a studio there for portrait-taking. That regency-striped chair, that table carved with a lion's face – where do they belong?

Most of the individual portraits, especially the early ones, are quite simply posed, but there are exceptions; for example James Balfour, who stands full length, one hand on hip in classic style, the other hand resting on the back of a chair with his top hat upended on the seat. His gloves dangle over the edge of the 'Egyptian' table, on which the wineglass with flowers in it has been placed. The brocade drapery hangs at one side of the doorway, with the door just visible, open. We're out of doors, of course – Hill and Adamson need the sun. Balfour looks a little ill-at-ease, stiff, a bit off-balance, but he has managed to hold still.

It's an interesting and complex portrait. But it's not the one Hill used when he painted Balfour in the Disruption picture. That can be found in a group of eight men. The photograph is splendidly dynamic – there's a lot going on. One man looks straight at the camera, others at some object in the distance. A young man at the front, with his elbow resting on a shiny top hat, makes a point with stabbing forefinger while his neighbour looks on. Another leans forward, distracted by something we can't see. Balfour stands at the back, his face in craggy profile, arm resting nonchalantly on the chair-back, ignoring all else while he contemplates infinity – as he does in Hill's painting.

After posing at Rock House, John Harden – who was impressed by Hill and Adamson's efficiency and the speed with which the business was done – strolled down the hill to see a celebrated painting currently being exhibited in Edinburgh, Sir George Hayter's vast canvas of the interior of the House of Commons begun in 1833 and showing the reformed parliament in session, crowded with figures. It was, said Harden, 'a wonderful production 10 years labour'.

Harden was so enchanted with the new art of calotype photography that he served as its apostle, telling his daughter that he would make a return visit to Rock House with John Wilson of Edinburgh University, alias 'Christopher North' of *Blackwood's Magazine*, whom he hoped to persuade to sit in front of the camera – 'a famous subject': 'Professor Wilson comes with me at two on Friday and I hope to get him to give five minutes'. The professor – an occasional neighbour of Harden in the Lake District, where both had homes – gave his five minutes; he appears in a calotype, burly, with his hair over his collar. Neither appears in the big picture. This is no surprise – Wilson was a Tory, and Harden had no ties with the Scottish Kirk.

But how the godly flocked to Hill and Adamson in quest of immortality on salt print, in oil paint!

They included the Rev. Horatio Bonar from Kelso, writer of religious poems; the Rev. Alexander Keith of St Cyrus, writer on prophecy; the Rev. John Forbes, mathematician; the Rev. John Longmuir, geologist and philologist; Gaelic scholar the Rev. Mackintosh Mackay, whose career path took him from Dunoon to Melbourne and Sydney; the Rev. John Lewis, of Leith and then Rome; the Rev. William King Hamilton of Stonehouse, hand on heart; Hugh Mackenzie of Tongue, smiling diffidently, soon to die. Snowy-headed George Muirhead of Cramond, oldest minister at the Assembly, with four years left to live; Dr Welsh with Bible, replaced in the big picture with a copy of the protest he read out at the Disruption assembly; the Rev. James Julius Wood in spectacles, but without them in the picture; Patrick Clason, clean-shaven in the calotype, bearded in the picture, as in later life; the Rev. James Grierson, minister at Errol, florid whiskers added in the picture; and many more.

While Hill and Adamson busied themselves with the fathers and brethren, they also found time for other sitters, some of whom were destined to appear in the painting, others not. Many were colleagues and cronies of the artist, painters like Horatio McCulloch, who stands with easel and brush in his hands; John (later Sir John) Steell, with thick curly hair, elbow on book with finger to cheek, hand stuck into his jacket, who sculpted Sir Walter Scott in marble for the monument in Princes Street; George Meikle Kemp, architect of the Scott Monument, calotyped shortly before he tumbled into the Union Canal on his homeward way one foggy night, probably with a drink in him. This was a sad loss: he drowned before he could see his gothic fantasy completed in all its glory. Kemp poses amid the rubble of the building work, clutching his scroll of plans.

Mostly the lay sitters are a more flamboyant lot than the clergymen, though some of the latter, too, can strike a suitably dramatic pose – to the pulpit born. John Blackie, who'd become Glasgow's lord provost, sticks chubby fingers into his striped waistcoat and quizzes the camera, with his hair falling over his brow and his beringed left hand lifted to shade his eye. Sultry-eyed George Baker is shown looking rakish in white waistcoat and spotted cravat, with tight pale-trousered thigh straddling the curled arm of the Rock House chair, fist to his head, cuffs showing, his other hand clasping a kerchief like a figleaf over his crotch. Dr George Bell, impressive in sepia tones, is seen to greater effect in the painting, elegant in a cream-coloured waistcoat and carelessly knotted blue and white-spotted necktie, beard streaked with grey.

Below Bell in the painting is David Octavius Hill himself, his sideburns, too, touched with time. Without doubt, Hill is the star of the calotype show, his own favourite model. Personal appearances before the camera are his forte – grave or gay, alone or with others, always natural, graceful, to the life. The first personality of the photographic art.

10

Through a lens, brightly

'I am much interested in the splendid discovery called Calotype', John Harden wrote to a female friend after sitting for his portrait at Rock House; 'single figures – groups – crowds – buildings – landscapes are all faithfully given and in a sepia-like drawing style of the most perfect truth ... it is indeed a marvellously great advance in Art and Scientific discovery'. Harden informed her that 'five minutes does the first or original likeness from which reduplication *many* can be produced without sitting again'. He added, however, that transferring the image from negative into finished print – the trickiest part of the process – took Adamson two or three days 'as sunshine serves'.

It's hard today to picture Adamson at work. Details are sketchy and he left no notes. A lot is left to conjecture. First, Adamson has to prepare his negative. He selects a suitable sheet of paper. He preferred a make of good-quality artist's paper called Whatman Turkey Mill – a paper with character, according to Sara Stevenson. It was also the paper the young aspiring artist Hill had used for his lithographs the of Perthshire landscape many years before. Sometimes, the watermark showed up on the negative – 'Whatman Turkey Mill' across the sky.

Next, he makes up various chemical solutions in which, in turn, he douses the paper sheet, drying it between immersions. A basic ingredient is silver in the form of silver nitrate, this being his essential light-sensitive material. Another step in the process is to coat the paper with a weak solution of common salt (sodium chloride) to improve its receptivity to light. Gallic acid, which speeds up the development of the image, is introduced at a later stage, along with other chemicals. All this is to some extent experimental; Adamson could, and no doubt did, vary the recipe according to the results he achieved.

Once his wash-and-dry programme is finished, Adamson has a negative – this negative being, strictly speaking, the calotype. The final photograph is correctly known as a salt, or salted, print.

To improve the translucence of the negative, Adamson may now smear it with wax and run a hot iron over it – an ordinary smoothing iron as used, no doubt, by his housekeeper – with a slot in the back to take a slug of hot lead. This done, he fits the paper negative into a wooden frame to make a rather clumsy slide. To save time, he can make up several slides for use the same day.

Now we go into the garden for the photo session. Adamson has set up the camera on its tripod, and the sitter is in position in front of the porch. Adamson bobs under the hood and removes the lens cap so that the light streams through, casting an image of the scene on the ground-glass sheet that forms the back of the camera. The picture he sees on the glass is in reverse and upside down, which to the unpractised eye takes a bit of getting used to. He adjusts the focus by sliding the lens back and forth until the topsy-turvy image is sharp. Now, perhaps, Hill may peer over his shoulder to make sure all's well, checking to see if any last-minute refinements should be made to the sitter's pose or the distribution of the props.

Adamson closes the lens cap again, removes the frosted glass at the back of the camera and in its place inserts the slide containing the negative. Maybe he looks at the sky to check the light – and to make sure no cloud is about to blot out the sun. The sky being clear, he removes the lens cap and takes the cover off the slide, allowing light to strike the treated paper negative. Watch in hand, he ticks off the seconds. Exposure can last from a few seconds to much longer – John Harden's five minutes is a long time to sit stock still.

Now Adamson has an exposed negative, which he will fix, wash and dry. At this point, his partner may want to mask flaws or make other improvements on the image. Impurities in the paper show up as a rash of dark spots on the negative. They may be caused by tiny bits of metal waste from the paper-milling machinery, or – since the paper was made of pulped rags, including old coats or shirts – particles of crushed metal buttons. Hill can dot with a pencil or brush out the flaws. Also, he has a chance to paint out unwanted details like the angle-braces and supports used to help the sitters keep still, and to define a line or touch up a feature with his pencil or brush. In a calotype of Robert Candlish, he added definition to the face and hair, and a wash over the shirt. One of his most significant alterations was to lengthen Hugh Miller's trademark plaid. He applied ink and watercolour to extend the garment so that it draped over the arm of his chair (as it does in the Disruption picture). He often pencilled contrast into a bland skyscape and, where necessary, got rid of the watermark.

So far, it has been relatively straightforward. Many photographers could get this far relatively easily. There's no mystery. But few could go on to make a successful salt print. The American writer on photography, Larry Schaaf, likens it to making fresh pasta: the ingredients are simple, but you need skill to bring it off. Adamson had the secret. Just what it was that gave him the edge over his competitors isn't known. As for Fox Talbot, the inventor of the calotype, his descriptions are tantalisingly vague. He probably worked as much by intuition, formed by trial and error, as by calculation.

Stage two. Adamson gets another frame, or slide, this one with a glass front. He takes a fresh sheet of paper, dips it in a salt solution and brushes it with silver nitrate, then puts it into the frame, places the negative on top, and the glass on top of that in a three-decker sandwich. Then it's out into the garden to place the slide in a sunny spot. The sun does its work, striking through glass and negative to imprint the image on the paper below.

Now Adamson has a positive. But still his work's not done. He has to dip it in a fixing solution, then wash it, and wash it again, and again; a tedious business, but, if he skimps, the print will fade. Brother John elaborated in an article on photography – though anonymous, it's assumed to be his – published in 1857, prescribing 'a most thorough and careful washing, in as many as twenty changes of water, over a period from eight to twelve hours, so as to remove if possible, all traces of the soluble compounds produced during the process'. Thomas Rodger, another of the old St Andrews circle, went even further. He recommended at least thirty hours of washing with 'incessant change of water and in two of those changes the water is made hot'.

The washing done, Adamson can sit back. He has a salt print at last. A photograph.

Adamson had a range of cameras to work with. The one he used most took pictures roughly eight by six inches (21 × 16cm). When he first teamed up with Hill, he had also used two smaller cameras, and later they acquired a larger one which could take photographs that were sixteen by thirteen inches, (43 × 33 cm). Essentially, they were empty wooden boxes with a lens fitted.

At least one and probably more of those cameras were made to order by Thomas Davidson of Edinburgh, who is usually described as an optician, though that barely gives an idea of the scope of his work. Davidson, a labourer's son from the north of England, was a skilled instrument-maker. Besides making cameras, he supplied Adamson and other early photographers working in Scotland with the chemicals they needed.

A metal daguerreotype camera thought to be made by Davidson is on show at the National Museum of Scotland in Edinburgh. It's unlike his box calotype cameras – more like a stumpy telescope. A calotype camera used by Talbot is on display beside it, and the difference is marked. Davidson, being a friend of Sir David Brewster, took his daguerreotyping apparatus to St Andrews, where he instructed the Brewster-John Adamson circle in its use.

Besides being hazy about the way Robert Adamson worked, we know distressingly little about the man himself. He left no account of his work, and, if he made practical notes of his experiments, they have not survived. His brother Dr John, who trained him, is almost as silent on the subject. Yet Adamson was the expert, the 'manipulator' as he was called, the scientist – far more than a technician – essential to the partnership. Hill would have been lost without him. 'I know nothing of the process though it is done under my nose,' he wrote, 'and I believe I never will.'

What Adamson thought or said is a blank. He's a shadowy figure, not much more than a latent image, a ghostly presence. The portrait which could have been made of him has faded beyond recall. We can imagine him in his lab, a room in Rock House, mixing the chemicals, sluicing his treated papers in the clear Edinburgh water (Fox Talbot was not so fortunate in his water supply), watching for the precise image to develop, with Hill possibly looking over his shoulder. Maybe Hill helped to bring out the furniture, the books and all the other props from the house. We think of Adamson setting up his camera on its tripod in the garden, peering through the eyepiece at the nervous sitters – all those black-coated ministers, or, better still, Hill's bohemian friends from the world of art and literature. Was he passive, a silent observer among them, or did he enjoy the crack as his partner did? Did he laugh and joke? There are no answers.

For a while, it was as if he had never been. When an international exhibition was held in Hill's old workplace, the Royal Scottish Academy, seven years after the artist's death, two albums were on show which the *Scotsman* described as 'a series of the artistic photographs produced many years ago by the late D. O. Hill'. No 'and Robert Adamson'. He'd been airbrushed out.

If Robert Adamson is hard to picture, the enigmatic Miss Mann is even more so. She emerges briefly in two letters to Hill written by James Nasmyth. 'How goes the divine solar art?' Nasmyth enquires jocularly in March 1847, 'and how does that worthy artist Mr Adamson the authentic contriver and manipulator in the art of light and darkness? and thrice worthy Miss Mann that most skilful and zealous of assistants?'

There's a shock. Up to now, there's been no hint of her or any other assistant. Yet Nasmyth goes on to say: 'I have the remembrance of All on Em so clearly calotyped in my mind's Eye as last I saw them in full manipulation of the divine art of light'. Who were *All* on Em? It's a puzzle. Perhaps Adamson, busy as he was, had recourse to other assistants, though, if so, no one seems to have thought them worth mentioning.

There has been speculation that, when the king of Saxony and his fellow travellers made a surprise visit to Rock House – probably encouraged to do so by Sir David Brewster, who had met the king's doctor – and had their photograph taken, it may have been 'manipulated' by Miss Mann. Adamson may have been absent. But that's guesswork. Recent research suggests that she was one of three sisters Mann – possibly her forename was Jessie – who lived close to Rock House at the time, but it's not certain.

Hill had immense regard for Adamson's talent, calling him 'the most successful manipulator the art has yet seen'. But respect for his ability was not the sole anchor of their working relationship. We can sense Hill's great affection for the younger man. They worked well together, and their partnership was amazingly productive. They seem to have been a perfect couple. They might have had a glittering future together. But, some months after Nasmyth's cheery reference to 'that worthy artist', Adamson, never robust, was struck down by ill-health. He fled the city to seek comfort in his birthplace by the sea, St Andrews, where he lingered briefly. He died there the following January. The fruitful partnership had lasted less than five years.

Hill, home from the graveside, penned a hasty and touching tribute: 'I have today assisted in consigning to the cold earth all that was earthly of my amiable true and affectionate Robert Adamson. He died in the full hope of a blessed resurrection. His truehearted family are mourning sadly especially his brother the Doctor – I have seldom seen such a deep & manly sorrow. Poor Adamson has not left his like in his art of which he was so modest.'

11

Flittings

Just before the Disruption, the good Dr Guthrie went visiting 'in a certain district of the country'. 'Is there no chance of a settlement?' he was asked by an anxious minister as they talked in the manse. Not a chance, replied Guthrie. 'We're certain to be out – as sure as the sunrise tomorrow.' As he said the words, Guthrie heard 'something like a groan' coming from an adjoining room. It came 'from the very heart' of the minister's wife, the mother of their family. Telling the story, Guthrie added: 'They had had many trials, there had been cradles and coffins in that home. The woman's heart was like to break.'

Before Hill completed his picture, the most famous, most talked-about painting of a Disruption scene was George Harvey's *Quitting the Manse*. Unlike Hill's grand historical canvas, it's a genre scene. Harvey pictured a dispossessed minister on the steps of his manse, supporting his aged mother on his arm and surrounded by his little children, while his wife turns the key in the lock of their home for the last time. Solemn villagers, labouring men and gentlefolk, are gathered around to say farewell, the men bareheaded, a peasant in the act of doffing his cap. Wide-eyed and implausibly angelic children look on. A farm cart with a few ears of corn still scattered on the boards stands ready to take the minister and his family away, and, in the gathering gloom, a wagon laden with their furniture can be seen rumbling along the road, with their cow tethered to its tailboard, past the old kirk silhouetted in the afterglow of the setting sun.

Harvey's picture drips with sentimentality. By the time he painted it, five years after the Disruption, the worst cases of hardship were past and a gloss of nostalgia could be applied. But for many Free Church adherents and their families, the reality had been harsh. For more than a few, the signing of the Deed of Demission had sentenced them and their wives and families to real hardship and suffering. There would be sickness and untimely death.

For Patrick MacFarlan, the central figure in Hill's painting and famously the most prosperous of the seceders, the quitting no doubt caused inconvenience and discomfort but was relatively painless. He left a spacious manse in Greenock but found a flat in town to move into, and he had an inherited estate to supplement his income. Four years before the Disruption, MacFarlan, recognising his relative good fortune, had remarked that it 'had pleased God to fill me a fuller cup than has fallen to any of my brethren'. Nevertheless, he said, he would rather throw 'that brimming cup away than drain it to the bitter dregs of apostasy'. Fine words.

John Swanson had to face discomfort and even peril on the sea. As pastor of the Small Isles – the islands of Eigg, Muck and Canna, south of Skye – Swanson spent much of his time sailing between the little communities scattered along those rocky coasts. When he came out at the Disruption, the absentee laird – a Dr McPherson of Aberdeen – turned him and his family out of the manse on Eigg, a comfortable place with several acres of glebe on which he kept a flock of sheep. The only home he could find for his wife and two small children was at Isle Oronsay, on the coast of Skye. Since this was too far up the sound to be convenient for his ministry, he had to spend long periods afloat on a sailing craft provided for him by the Free Kirk.

This was the small sailing vessel *Betsey*, skippered by Swanson himself, who must have been a good seaman to handle the ageing craft in those rough and treacherous waters. Hugh Miller, his friend since schooldays in Cromarty, spent several weeks sailing with him on his rounds; and, since Miller was at his best writing about the sea and the open sky and natural world, his account comes across with the zest of a yarn well told. But the life must have been serious enough for Swanson. Writing in the *Witness* at the time of the Disruption, Miller had eulogised Swanson as an exemplary parish minister. Now he made a damning comparison with the previous incumbent in the Small Isles, a man called Donald Maclean. His problem was drink.

When Miller came to write an account of his visit to the Small Isles with Swanson in his book *The Cruise of the Betsey*, he told of making his way past a ruinous building on Eigg which had formerly been the public house. Maclean, according to Miller, had been its best customer: 'He was in the practice of sitting in one of its dingy little rooms, day after day, imbibing whisky and peat-reek'. Eventually, Maclean was summoned before the Kirk, where he foolishly flaunted his sins: 'Had not the infatuated man got senselessly drunk one evening, when in Edinburgh on his trial, and staggered, of all places in the world, into the General Assembly, he would probably have died minister of Eigg'. Maclean was summarily dismissed. A year after his humiliation, he died on board a steamer in the Firth of Clyde, at the age of forty-six.

Swanson in his sea-going ministry was the very picture of a mariner. Miller described him coming aboard – a 'skipper-like man' in a pea jacket – with his mate, the Gaelic-speaking John Stewart, who was clad in a guernsey smock. An unnamed young deckhand made up the complement. Miller reflected on the good fortune of Swanson 'aboard his Free Church yacht, which, if not very secure when nights were dark and winds loud, and the little vessel tilted high to the long roll of the Atlantic, lay at least beyond the reach of man's intolerance'. She was clinker-built and a sturdy sea-going vessel, though she was beginning to show her age. She was, Miller said, describing her appearance on a fine day, 'evidently a thing of high spirit', tall-masted 'with a smart rake aft, and a spruce outrigger astern, and flaunting her triangular flag of blue in the sun'.

Miller, on holiday from his editorial duties in the *Witness* office, eagerly grasped the opportunity to geologise at their landfalls. He made two cruises on the *Betsey*, the first, of six weeks, in July and August 1844, the second a year later. 'Chisels and hammers, and the bag for specimens, were taken from their corner in the dark closet', he wrote, along with a stock of 'a fine *soft* Conservative Edinburgh newspaper, valuable for a quality of preserving old things entire'. Stowing all this away could not have been easy, according to his own description of the cramped quarters aboard.

The cabin was 'about twice the size of a common bed, and just lofty enough under the beams to permit a man of five feet eleven to stand erect in his nightcap'. It had a little iron stove with two seats in front of it, and a table lashed to the floor with a writing desk on top. There was just enough room to squeeze between the table and the bunks – which reminded Miller of coffins – along the side. There was a barred skylight with a lantern hanging from it which cast only a feeble light below on dark nights.

Miller remarked on the curious mixture of sacred and secular material heaped on or around the table. There was a well-thumbed chart of the Western Isles, an equally well-used Bible commentary, a 'polyglot' – a bilingual bible in both Gaelic and English – a telescope in the corner, a copy of Calvin's *Institutes*, and the latest edition of *The Coaster's Sailing Directions*. Next to the cabin was what Miller called a state room, just about large enough to take an armchair if an armchair could be got through the door. Here, Miller saw Swanson's printing press and case of types. Miller didn't explain why the minister needed to be a printer as well. Possibly he wrote and distributed tracts. Hanging above the press was the vessel's blue ensign with the words 'Free Church Yacht' boldly displayed on it.

A door led by a low passage to the forecastle, a cubicle which served as galley, with a glowing fire in it and the chain cable dangling from the hatchway. Here Miller saw the handsome young deckhand squatting in front of the blaze, with sleeves rolled up and his shirt open at the breast, 'like the household goblin described by Milton'. On Miller's arrival, sometime after midnight, John Stewart, crouching low as he came from the galley, brought him a plateful of fresh herring 'splendidly toasted'.

The island folk were solicitous for the welfare of their minister. Wherever the *Betsey* stopped, there were gifts of provisions – on one occasion, three bottles of cream were sent from the shore along with 'oaten cakes' made on the island from ingredients in the ship's store (oatmeal was scarce on Eigg in July). On their way to a religious meeting on shore, they stopped at a cottage and were given a bowl of creamy milk and 'a splendid platter of mashed potatoes, and we dined like princes'. Islanders on Rum left them a basket filled with half a dozen new-caught trout and a pail of razor fish.

When they called at Isle Oronsay, with the chance of a brief visit to Swanson's wife and family, whom he hadn't seen for a month, 'a kind friend' sent on board what Miller jocularly called 'two pieces of rare antiquity, two bottles of semi-fossil Madeira'. Once at sea again, no puritan sense of self-denial inhibited them from sampling the wine, and the bouquet 'filled the cabin with fragrance every time the cork was drawn'.

One day, as usual on a Saturday, Swanson kept to his cabin preparing for his sermon for the Sabbath. Miller amused himself by fishing, but caught nothing, then took to the dinghy and 'sent half a dozen pistol bullets after a shoal of porpoises'

– to no effect. (One of Miller's eccentricities was his habit of carrying a loaded pistol about his person.) The light winds of the morning gave way to a flat calm, and then, in the evening, the weather broke. 'The gale, thickened with rain, came down, shrieking like a maniac, from off the peaked hills of Rum. But the *Betsey*, with her storm-jib set, and her mainsail reefed to the cross, kept her weather bow bravely to the blast.' Having been the pleasure yacht of 'a man of fortune' accustomed to riding out severe weather in the Bay of Biscay, old *Betsey* 'had now got somewhat crazy in her fastenings, and made rather more water in a heavy sea than her one little pump could conveniently keep under'.

That night, Swanson got little sleep since 'we had no other such helmsman aboard'; but at least the only mishap was the loss of his sou'wester, torn away by the wind. The following day, after taking services ashore, he returned exhausted and, said Miller, 'the sternest teetotaller in the kingdom would scarce have forbidden him a glass of our fifty-year-old Madeira'. Whether or not he took his glass, and what were its effects, Miller doesn't say, but his overtired friend took to his bed with 'an excruciating headache', lying with eyes shut but sleepless, rocked by the swell.

On his second cruise on the *Betsey*, Miller and Swanson faced a worse hazard. Running in rough seas, the *Betsey* sprang a leak, and only a desperate manning of the pump and baling with buckets kept her afloat, and her crew from drowning.

In general, ministers in towns and cities fared better than their rural brethren, where the hostility of patrons and unsympathetic landowners could, and did, lead not just to discomfort but to catastrophe. Their tribulations were recorded comprehensively forty years later by Robert Brown in his *Annals of the Disruption*. Thomas Guthrie, who travelled round the country just after the

Disruption to report on the situation, provides a contemporary eyewitness account of some of the worst cases.

He found tragedy in the far north with the Mackenzies, father and son. The fine manse at Tongue on the northern shoreline had been occupied by the Mackenzie family for nearly 100 years, but had to be given up at the Disruption. Most of the family moved to Thurso, forty miles away; but the patriarch, seventy-two-year-old Hugh Mackenzie, and his son who acted as his assistant and expected to succeed him in the ministry there, stayed on in the neighbourhood. The only accommodation they could find was a room and bed-closet in a mean little cottage. When Guthrie called on them early one morning, he found them both ill with a fever. Guthrie walked in to discover the old man slumped in a chair, his white hairs awry, sound asleep after passing a tormented night. Thinking it wrong to wake him, he turned to the son who was lying haggard in the bed nook in the corner. He too had been unable to sleep; he said his father's groans 'were like daggers in his heart'. 'My father's conscience and mine are at peace', the younger man said.

It was well. The old man died that summer, and the son followed him some weeks later – martyrs, as Guthrie thought, 'for those great principles for which we abandoned our earthly all', and gone 'to the place where the wicked cease from troubling and the weary are at rest' – conventional words, maybe, from a man whose Biblical eloquence flowed like a mother tongue, but none the less moving. It brought tears to Guthrie's eyes; he was 'never so unmanned by any sight'. Leaving the cottage, he said, 'I felt my corruption rising'.

At the other end of the country, at Cockburnspath on the Berwickshire coast, he paid a winter visit to a Mr Baird, finding him in a plain but and ben – a two-room cottage – with a small cellar below ground and a garret under the rafters. The walls were damp, and no fire could be lit in the closet. Baird showed him his 'study', climbing 'a sort of trap-stair' to the garret which boasted a chair, table and a flock bed, a few inches above which were bare slates 'as white with hoar frost within as they were white with snow without'. Next morning, Baird confessed that he hadn't closed an eye for the cold: 'his very breath on the blankets was frozen as hard as the ice outside'. Baird soon succumbed, and once again Guthrie called to mind Covenanting times: 'That man lies in a martyr's grave'.

Compared with these tragic cases, the condition in which Dr Henry Duncan found himself was relatively fortunate. A courteous and much-loved man, best known for starting the savings bank movement, he was forced, in his seventieth year, to leave his comfortable manse in the parish of Ruthwell, near Annan in Dumfriesshire. Wellwishers rallied round to clean, scrub and whitewash the damp, smoky and partly unroofed cottage which he and his wife now occupied on the Dumfries-Carlisle turnpike road, overshadowed by an ugly quarry. A kind neighbour made a gate in a hedge so that he and his wife could stroll in the field, or read their books in fine weather among the plots of wild rose and honeysuckle.

Duncan was no firebrand. Early in his career he'd been a Moderate, but he'd come round to support the Kirk's veto act, and he'd written a lengthy letter to his old friend Henry Brougham – the Lord Brougham who'd incurred Hugh Miller's wrath – advocating reform of the Kirk and a curb on patronage. Lord Melbourne, as home secretary, had received another of his missives. Duncan was urbane and well connected, counting Thomas Chalmers as a warm friend. He was a cultured man with a taste for antiquities who found and restored an ancient runic cross. This became a focal point in the manse garden he'd transformed – so it was said – into a paradise.

Guests visiting his new home – one room, a kitchen and a bed-closet – were puzzled when he invited them into his drawing room. This turned out to be the 'great drawing room of nature': he led them into the deserted quarry at the back of the cottage, where he'd planted young trees on heaps of rubble, with winding paths and a rustic bridge made by his own hands which spanned two standing pools. Duncan had little time in which to enjoy this lesser paradise. He suffered a stroke while taking a prayer meeting and died shortly after. Maybe his enforced flitting and his damp living quarters contributed to his death – who can tell? Other cases of illness and death among the exiled Free Kirk families might be attributed to their unhealthy quarters.

David Brown, minister at Roslin, a village near Edinburgh, found shelter for his family in two tiny cottages side by side. There were better places to be had for rent in the neighbourhood, but the landlord forbade his tenants to take them in. One of the twin cottages, a single room with a bare earth floor inadequately covered with a piece of felt, served as bedroom. As one scrap of felt rotted, another had to be bought from the paper mill nearby. At bedtime, the family had to decamp from damp living room to chilly bedroom next door. Not surprisingly, the minister's health broke down.

Roderick Mackay and his family made several flittings from one bad home to another in Skye. After the last, a visitor found Mackay's 'six or seven' children crammed into one small room. Mackay spoke of 'the fell disease that has made my company so desolate', a pregnant phrase that implies the death of loved ones – a child, perhaps, or wife.

Mr McVean, minister at Iona, and his family were forced to live in an old house across the sound used for many years as a granary, a cold and draughty place where the family took ill and a child died. The distraught father found lodging for his family in the schoolmaster's house until the teacher was 'so severely handled by his presbytery' – established churchmen in want of Christian charity – that McVean had to leave. Declining to move to the town of Tobermory, fifty-five miles away on the other side of Mull, McVean at last took shelter in 'one of the most miserable huts on the shore'. Here he was found by Dr Merle d'Aubignon of Geneva, a leader of the Swiss Protestant church and a staunch ally of the Free Kirk. D'Aubignon was moved to tears.

Thomas Davidson, minister at Kilmallie, in Lochaber, and his wife and children thought themselves well off in rooms at Annat House, but their good fortune ran out and they had to move into a hut only twelve feet square, and so leaky that they had to stuff blankets into the cracks and holes in the walls in an attempt to keep out the wind and rain. A third move saw them in two rooms in the ferry house, but not for long. 'Even this they had to give up', notes Brown in his *Annals*. Mrs Davidson fell ill, and, early in 1847, husband and wife left for Glasgow to seek medical aid. But she died two months later; according to Davidson, she was 'another victim to the cruel oppression of the proprietors of Scotland'.

Mr Campbell of Berriedale in Caithness couldn't warm the chill in his bones as he huddled by his fireside happed in a greatcoat. The old ruined cottage, amateurishly roofed by the schoolteacher with whom he shared lodging, was damp and cold. After a night of heavy rain he'd find a pool of water at the foot of his bed, and, on windy nights, downdraught on the dying fire blew ashes in his face. As the cottage had been built on a heap of stones, the wind whistled up through the floorboards. He took to walking out of doors in an attempt to stop the swelling in his feet caused by the damp, and, as year followed year in the hovel, he feared for his life.

One night he woke in alarm, disturbed by a clattering 'very like the noise of people in danger of shipwreck on the seashore' – sounds familiar to a pastor among fishing folk. He could hear men shouting above the tumult of the gale, and when he roused himself he discovered neighbours had rallied round to secure his roof from blowing away. But blow away it did, leaving his bed curtains flapping like sails in the storm. He and the teacher then set about building a house and a school (hopefully on a better plan) and then, eager to have a sound roof over their head, hastily moved in before the walls had been plastered.

John Kirk, ousted from his manse in the village of Arbirlot, found accommodation in Arbroath, several miles away. Three and a half years later, he calculated that he had covered nearly 2,000 miles on foot, walking there and back on his pastoral duties. One cold stormy night, he set off home at nine o'clock after a kirk meeting, thinking the wind and rain had abated. But, as he tramped the long miles, the downpour resumed, drenching him to the skin, and he struggled to keep upright in the teeth of the gale. In the darkness, he came on a crowd of navvies. The gusts dashed him from one navvy to another, but they took it in good part. He arrived home at eleven, worn out by the adventure.

Feelings ran high, and friendships were broken at the Disruption. The Rev. Colin Mackenzie of Shieldaig, in Wester Ross, had respite for a few months: the church was barred to him, but he was permitted to occupy the manse for a few months while he tried, vainly, to find a house in the neighbourhood for himself, his elderly mother and two other family members. He wrote to the laird at Applecross House, a relative who had been a boyhood friend and was now a member of parliament. After several refusals of help, he called on the man in his mansion as a last resort. He got a chilly welcome and a harangue for his pains. He was called a fool for bringing his family to beggary, and just at the time when the laird was minded to promote him to a better living – a fine example of patronage in action. Furthermore, he must immediately quit the manse, the parish and the whole Shieldaig estate – and if he did not, the laird would make sure he regretted it. No tenant would be allowed to offer him so much as a room in a cottage.

One concession was made: for that night only, he might receive what the laird was pleased to call 'Highland hospitality' in 'a miserable inn not far from the mansion'. As a parting shot, he was ordered to be off after breakfast, and never to darken the laird's door again. Henceforth he would be recognised as neither pastor nor friend.

12

Kirk without a steeple

Early in 1846, a set of large prints headed *Illustrations of the Principles of Toleration in Scotland* went on sale in Edinburgh, Glasgow, Manchester, Liverpool and London. There was heavy irony in the title. What the pictures illustrated was the intolerance of landlords who not only refused to allow Free Kirk people to worship in the local church but also denied them any sites on which to build a new church of their own. The 'principles of toleration' of the title was borrowed from an edict of the French Revolution allowing dissidents the right of worship – it was not observed!

The Preface explained that all the 'engravings' (actually, lithographs) had been made from drawings made on the spot, and were faithful representations of places where congregations of the Free Church had assembled for worship in consequence of 'determined and reiterated refusal on the part of proprietors to grant on any terms ground for sites for their churches'. After three years of patient suffering,

> it has occurred to some friends of religious liberty to adopt the present mode of making known to the public the nature and extent of an abuse which, short of ocular proof, could scarcely be believed to exist in Great Britain in the nineteenth century, in the hope that such publicity may aid them in their efforts to obtain from the legislature what they have been unable to obtain from the toleration, humanity, or justice of individual proprietors.

Three artists were engaged on the project. David Octavius Hill contributed two illustrations and James Drummond several others. All illustrations were lithographed by Andrew Maclure, a number of them from his own original sketches. Hill's *Open-air Worship at Wanlockhead* was the best and most dramatic.

The village of Wanlockhead — at 1,500 feet above sea level, the highest in Scotland — is situated in steep, featureless hills in the Southern Uplands. At that time, most of the male inhabitants worked in the lead mines, which, like all the surrounding country, belonged to the Duke of Buccleuch. It was a harsh environment in winter, swept by gales and blizzards. The passes were often blocked. In wintertime, the miners barely saw daylight, going to work in the dark mornings and emerging from the clammy underground tunnels into the dark of evening. They had a hard life, equipping them, possibly, for the rigours of five years when they had to worship in the open.

The text appended to the print explained that, though the parish church was eight miles away in the town of Sanquhar at the bottom of the glen, a chapel for the local people had been built in the village many years before. As Wanlockhead was an outpost of the vast Buccleuch properties, the duke felt he could regulate his villagers' worship as well as controlling their work, and since he was bitterly hostile to the Free Kirk he gave no concessions to the 280 parishioners who left the establishment at the Disruption. They were out in the cold. Buccleuch ignored all requests addressed to him personally for permission to build. Thomas Chalmers wrote and got no answer. Further pleas to the duke's factor received a curt refusal. So, for five years, the congregation had to meet in some cranny or other in the hills, changing ground when necessary according to the vagaries of the winds.

Hill's winter journey to remote Wanlockhead cannot have been easy. Possibly he took the train to Abington in the Clyde valley and then some kind of horse transport up the steep and winding pass through the hills. Once there, he either witnessed or imagined a storm sweeping down the glen as the villagers hastened to the place of worship. In his representation of the scene, a squall of sleet or snow slants across the hills, and a fierce wind tugs at skirts and plaids as the faithful lean forward into the gale, clutching hats and bonnets to their heads. One man carries two stools. In the middle distance, a small crowd gathers round a makeshift pulpit, on to which a stray beam of light has momentarily fallen. The dark barrier of huge hills dominates the puny mortals, and a ravine drops down to the river below. A line of trestles and the mouth of a mine cut into the hillside indicate the industry of the place.

Visiting preachers left their own descriptions of Sunday worship at Wanlockhead (always, it seems, in inclement weather): 'The wooden erection which served for a pulpit was placed at the bottom of the hollow, and the people sat most of them on stones upon the side of the hill, and some round the minister on chairs which they had brought. The service lasted an hour and three-quarters. I was quite wet through.' Another described his congregation 'ranged on the side of the mountain. It was a swampy place … The people were standing on the wet grass, and there were showers lashing – what they call hill showers – and they were exposed to the storm and rain.' A third minister, on a bitter day of frost and snow, found his legs so numbed by the end of the service that he had to be helped from the stone he stood on.

Wanlockhead was not the only country place where the devout had only 'the canopy of heaven' over their heads. There were many more. Hill sketched a gathering at Canonbie, 'on the Scotch side of the English border' – another community owing allegiance to the Duke of Buccleuch, and no better treated. People are seated round the young minister in a grove of leafless trees. One seems to be counting the collection, with his dog at his side, and a horse waits patiently for its master.

Andrew Maclure drew the scene at Duthil, in Strathspey, where he pictured the people standing in a hollow thinly studded with pine trees. The landowner there was the Earl of Seafield, another proprietor of large estates who steadfastly refused his tenants shelter even in the severest weather. Maclure was also at Ballater with his sketchpad, where the people at first spent the winter 'on a muir in that high and stormy district'. But in his sketch a motley group of people clad in plaids, shawls, bonnets and hats are gathered outside a mean little building. This was a low-walled sheep-cot (only five feet high, and no more than nine feet wide) some distance from the village. It was small but, as the text says, preferable in winter to meeting in the open air.

At Kilmallie on the west coast, the people barred from the kirk at first gathered in the kirkyard among the headstones, but after several Sundays there they were ordered out, and found a 'little green spot' on the shore just above the high-tide mark. At Humbie in East Lothian, a deep wooded ravine provided a meeting place. A field at the Lanarkshire village of Lesmahagow offered by a local surgeon friendly to the Free Kirk although he was not an adherent proved an ideal spot, gently sloping and partly sheltered by trees on three sides. At the 'lord's supper' – the communion service – worshippers brought chairs or 'rustic seats' while others sat on the bare ground round the supper laid out on the grass.

A communion scene on the island of Mull was drawn by James Drummond for the *Principles of Toleration*. The ceremony took place in a gravel pit on bare moorland. A few trees bend to the wind. Most of the congregation stand in the open, but, through the opening of a small tent erected under the bank, the minister can be glimpsed holding up the goblet, with a handful of communicants seated around him.

Outdoor settings such as these could be strangely solemn. At Helmsdale, where Hugh Miller joined some 800 worshippers in the open, he was struck by the plaintive singing of psalms in Gaelic – 'even more melancholy than usual'.

Occasionally, when the weather was fine, alfresco worship may have had something of the feeling of a country picnic about it. In fact, the weather seems to have been reasonably kind for the first months after the Disruption. A Mr Grant, an amateur meteorologist, took careful notes at his home in the Perthshire village of Braco and observed that, although the spring had been unusually wet, not a drop of rain fell on the sabbath for the next four and a half months. Some of the devout took this to be a sign of divine providence. But it could be touch and go. Hugh Miller woke several times during one stormy Saturday night of broken sleep to hear rainwater gushing from the eaves and pattering furiously on the window panes of his lodging in Cromarty. He feared for the poor worshippers likely to be exposed to the fury of the storm when morning came. But the rain stopped and he woke to a sky crossed only by a host of ragged clouds careering before the easterly wind. It was dry!

'God's answers to prayers were most striking', declared the minister at Blairgowrie. 'Often on Saturdays the rain poured in torrents, but by Sabbath the sun and wind were sent.' Here and there, God turned a deaf ear. After many dry sabbaths, an ominous dark cloud spread across the sky over the field at Lesmahagow, and down came the deluge. Rain drummed so loudly on raised umbrellas that the minister could hardly hear his own voice, and his big pulpit Bible was almost ruined. Ever after, he cherished the permanently rain-daubed pages as a memorial of the times.

At Crailing in Roxburghshire, the sky suddenly grew black over the Cheviot hills, and loud peals of thunder crashed over-head. The minister was equal to the occasion: he scrapped his text and preached a sermon on the voice of God. Service over, and still dry, the people hastened home, reaching shelter just as the 'most terrific storm burst'.

Such storms were exceptional. Mostly the sun shone, and the harvest was golden. A farmer grateful for this blessing arranged the haystacks in his yard in a circle so that the Free Kirk folk could meet within their sheltering corral. And when a visitor to Muckhart, in Clackmannanshire, commented on the number of farmers' vehicles he saw roll past carrying building material donated for the new Free Kirk, he was told that 'God has given it all back' – not in any spiritual uplift, as he supposed, but in cash.

Inevitably the spell of fine weather broke, and winter brought new trials for the outed congregations. The minister appointed to preach at Rannoch in October on 'the most inclement day of the season' could find nowhere to hold the service except on the loch shore. The wind drowned his voice at times, and spray torn from the waves wet the huddled people.

Fortunate congregations found buildings of a sort in lieu of a church. Barns were popular. Elderly Michael Stirling, forced to quit the church at Cargill, Perthshire, where he had preached for thirty-four years, walked down among a throng of his supporters, 'bearing the sacred volume beneath his arm', to their makeshift kirk, a barn at Newbiggin. Since the barn was too small to accommodate them all, those left outside gathered round the open door, joined in the praise – and some wept as they craned to hear the old man's tremulous discourse. Elsewhere, at a place called Corich, a wool barn served well except for some weeks in July when it was filled with wool from the sheep-shearing.

Stables served. At Fairlie on the Firth of Clyde, a wellwisher fitted up her stable with forms and a pulpit which had 'come into her possession' after being preached from in Liverpool by a celebrated evangelist. A large new stable for six horses with a hay loft above it was made use of in Stanley, Perthshire. It had been built by a gentleman lately returned from making his fortune in America. 'Commercial convulsions' in the States later required him to recross the Atlantic, but the congregation was allowed to stay.

The people at Monikie, in Angus, worshipped for nine years in a grain loft, with hardly any headroom under the slates – a good sounding board for psalm-singing if nothing else. At Oyne, in Aberdeenshire, snow filtered through crannies in the roof of a cart shed on to bowed heads; the old folk found it particularly distressing. Bits of timber were put together to make a crude shelter in a saw pit near Gareloch, 'but most of us sat *sub jove*' (in the open) – as Robert Rainy, then a lad, remembered long afterwards when he was a college principal.

Where a site could be had and timber was available, temporary wooden kirks were built, like the 'Tabernacle' at Largo. One appeared at Woodside in Aberdeen, another in Ayr. There, infestations of beetles, earwigs and mice annoyed the worshippers; also, rain seeped through the roof in wet weather, and drops of melted pitch oozed through in a heatwave. The people of Rhynie, Aberdeenshire, and friends from afar assembled early one Saturday at a plot on the outskirts of the village as cartloads of building materials arrived. Their title to the place was dubious, but they set to work, and 'before the shades of evening fell' they had raised a plain but substantial wooden church, where the Saturday labourers worshipped on Sunday. In the neighbouring parish of Bellie, fifty carpenters from Garmouth turned up for work on the Tuesday, and by the sabbath eve the church was built.

Many workers, like the Garmouth carpenters, gave their services gratis. Goods were supplied free or at reduced charge. Dressed timber was presented by a merchant for a congregation near Beauly, Inverness-shire. There, for five days, squads of workmen turned up with their tools to clear stones and whin bushes and level the ground for the Gaelic congregation, and to build a church for the English-speakers. A congregation of

2,000 heard the minister preach in Gaelic in the open on the Sunday forenoon, and, that afternoon, he switched to English for the 400 people packed into the new wooden kirk, with an overflow standing outside.

Tents were another solution. Even as the Disruption Assembly met, a smart London entrepreneur had arrived in Edinburgh, offering tents for sale. He was not the only source of supply. The Free Kirk arranged for the supply of lightweight tents (no more than four hundredweight) to be easily transportable by cart or small boat. Soon tents sprang up all over the country.

To his surprise and delight, the minister at Blairgowrie, north of Dundee, returned from the Assembly to find a large tent pitched on ground adjoining the glebe – never mind that it was a patchwork affair stitched together from odd canvas sails, both black and white, donated by a Dundee shipowner. It seated 1,000 on close-packed benches covered in white cotton cloth. A thick layer of sawdust muffled the minister's steps as he walked down the narrow aisle that Sunday, preceded by his glebe servant acting as beadle and carrying the Bible. Psalm 100 was sung: 'O enter then his gates with praise'; and indeed the Lord was felt to be present.

At Gifford, East Lothian, at a pleasant situation beside a waterfall, the local wright constructed supporting walls with two cartloads of wood thinnings sent by a local gentleman from his estate; when roofed with strong cloth, this structure housed 500. But tents were not immune in all weathers. After their spell on the open shore, worshippers at Kilmallie spent the first three months of 1845 in a large canvas tent pitched nearby. Sadly it proved temporary. On 30 March a violent storm ripped the canvas from the wooden slabs supporting it. Services continued to be held for more than two years in this roofless enclosure, in all weathers, until first a wooden shed and then, at last, a church was built.

At Durness on the north coast, with a clear view of the Orkney Islands on a fine day, a tent was pitched in a gravel pit a quarter of a mile from the sea. A fierce snowstorm broke during the service on 18 February, and, as the minister spoke to his congregation, the canvas was suddenly rent from top to bottom. Young men accustomed to manning sailing vessels took hold of the wildly flapping canvas and managed to lash it to the poles. Making the best of it, the minister hunched his back to the blast, covered his head in his handkerchief and proceeded with his sermon while his audience 'crouched a little closer to each other and adjusted their cloaks and plaids'. The sea's margin, it was said, was a continuous line of foam and spray, and waves thundered on shore. Yet, as the writer of *Annals* wryly commented, as those people cowered under the lash of the storm, the unrelenting laird who had denied them a place to build a shelter 'was perhaps worshipping the same God under the roof of some aisled and groined cathedral in his cushioned pew, his eyes delighted with dim religious light, and his ears regaled with the sounds of the solemn organ'.

In his *Cruise of the Betsey*, Hugh Miller tells of a church service held in what he described as 'a low dingy cottage of turf and stone' on the island of Eigg. The weather was bad as the vessel *Betsey*, skippered by his friend John Swanson, minister of the Small Isles, put into the bay on the Sunday morning. Thick mist lay over the hills, and rain streamed down. The two men landed and set off for the meeting place, Swanson 'encased in his ample-skirted storm-jacket of oiled canvas' and Miller closely wrapped in his grey maud or plaid which, for all its properties, failed to keep out the wet, no proof 'against the penetrating powers of a true Hebridean drizzle'.

There was irony in the meeting place. Not only did it stand nearly opposite the windows of the snug manse Swanson had been forced to leave, but it had been built by him at his own expense to serve as a Gaelic school. 'The rude turf-building we found full from end to end, and all a-steam with a particularly wet congregation, some of whom, neither very robust nor young, had travelled in the soaking drizzle from the farthest extremities of the island'. The roughly made pulpit where Swanson preached was 'grotesquely rude', the makeshift pews were unplaned deals set on the uneven earth floor, and rain coursed down the two small windows. Swanson preached in Gaelic, which Miller did not know, then gave a brief digest in English 'for the benefit of his one Saxon auditor'.

The arrival of the *Betsey* in the offing acted as a church bell. On one occasion as they rounded the headland, Miller saw people 'wending their way, in threes and fours, through the dark moor, to the place of worship – a black turf hovel. The appearance of the *Betsey* in the loch had been a gathering signal.'

One of James Drummond's illustrations in *Principles of Toleration* shows a cluster of people on the hillside overlooking Loch Sunart, listening to their young minister who addresses them from a kind of tepee (poles made from the stems of slender trees poke through an opening at the top). A corner of the loch is visible behind him, with boats pulled up on the shore and a thatched cottage above the shoreline with smoke curling from a hole in the roof. The hills in the background are capped with snow.

The print is headed *Strontian, Loch Sunart* – Strontian being a village on the north side of the loch, on the Ardnamurchan peninsula. One of the most ingenious temporary kirks found an anchorage here – the famous floating kirk of Ardnamurchan. Money was raised, with a contribution from David Octavius Hill in the form of an illustration for the prospectus, and an order placed with a yard on the Clyde. The vessel was simply a large box set on an iron barge – a container ship of the day. A couple of steam paddle tugs hauled the unwieldy craft down the Firth of Clyde and round the Mull of Kintyre into the Atlantic. Passing through the sounds of Jura and Mull, it reached the safety of Loch Sunart after a tricky voyage, for twice it slewed out of control and swept towards rocks. Folk knowledgeable about sailing surveyed the coast and identified the most suitable moorage; but, since this lay under the windows of the laird Sir James Riddell, a determined opponent of the Free Kirk, it was tactfully decided to anchor some two miles away, about 150 yards offshore.

On Sundays, the loch was thick with small sailing and rowing boats as people made their way towards the vessel. Others came striding across the hills from as far as eight or nine miles distant, and even further in summer. Ropes were strung out between shore and vessel to ease the passage from dry land, but, even so, boarding could be awkward, particularly in rough seas. When fully loaded, more than 600 could be squeezed aboard. A gauge at the bow enabled a rough calculation to be made – for every hundred on board, the boat sank an inch in the water. They sat on benches laid across the beam. The minister remarked on the pleasant 'swashy' noise to be heard as the waves rippled against the hull.

Throughout the day, with two services in Gaelic and one in English to be got through, the weather might change dramatically, from flat calm to an unpleasant choppiness. At the end of the day, even at the best of times, it took a long time to get all safely ashore. Even in summer, the last to make land would be trudging home in the gloaming, and it would be dark before they got there.

Meanwhile, the building of permanent churches went ahead. Plans had been made well in advance. On the eve of the Disruption, Thomas Chalmers was pleased to report that the building fund already stood at £180,000. Donations had come from high and low, and not just in cash. Two 'friends of the evangelicalism of the Church of Scotland' had contributed £15; a 'Scotchwoman in Ireland' £1. Women dipped into their jewel boxes. 'A lady, a friend to the Free Presbyterian Church of Scotland' donated a gold ring; a Highland lady a gold brooch, a pair of bracelets and a buckle. A lady from St Andrews gave her handsome gold chain and cross, plus gold earrings.

Rigorous economy had to be observed, as Chalmers explained. Six or seven hundred churches had to be built, but conventional building with stone and lime and slates was out of the question – too expensive. The materials would be brick, wood and roofing felt, as in the church already built for Candlish in Lothian Road. And there would be no frills, which meant, among other things, no steeples. A popular jingle of the day expressed it from the Free Kirk point of view:

> The Free Kirk, the wee kirk,
>   the kirk without a steeple.
> The auld kirk, the cauld kirk,
>   the kirk without the people.

That was too partisan. The Free Kirk by no means had over-whelming support among the people. It was strong in the Highlands, but more evenly spread elsewhere; and in some areas – the Borders, for example – it was in a definite minority.

Self-help came into play, as at Tobermory where a site was got and, once a good source of stone had been found, the local people set to quarrying, blasting and digging the foundations under the eye of 'two aged and experienced tradesmen'. No-one 'found guilty of taking excess of ardent spirits, or swearing of any kind' was to be taken on. Boatmen shipped in lime and gravel without charging freight. Masons, some with horse and cart, offered a week's work free. Labourers who could only afford a week or so without pay got square meals for their pains.

At Muthill, in Perthshire, two masons appointed to scour the country for building sand spotted a huge heap of stones in a field almost hidden by young trees. They reckoned that even such 'great coarse boulders of the most unpromising kind' could be used. Take them, said the proprietor – 800 cartloads.

The poor state of the building industry helped greatly – wages and the price of materials were low, and men were out of work. It was said that a few years later it would have cost 30 per cent more to build the same number of churches.

In spite of the austerity rule, some handsome buildings were put up – the finest said to be in Aberdeen, where a group of three churches, when observed from Union Bridge, had the 'aspect of a cathedral'. The style was simple lancet gothic, but there was a lofty square tower and – for once – a spire.

13

Dreams and visions

When David Octavius Hill published his set of engravings of *The Land of Burns*, three years before the Disruption, he included a whimsical frontispiece. The setting is a gothic archway at the ruined Lincluden Abbey near Dumfries, 'yon roofless tower' where the poet imagined himself falling asleep and meeting – but who else? – 'a lassie all alone'. Burns, oblivious to the waking world, reclines in the foreground with his head in the lap of his bewitching muse – made drowsy, Hill suggests, by 'partaking too freely' of recent hospitality.

High above, outlined against a full moon, an aged bard plucks at his clarsach. Ostensibly he is 'the stern and stalwart ghaist' of Liberty, but he also brings to mind both the harpist in Scott's *Lay of the Last Minstrel*, whose

> withered cheek, and tresses gray,
> Seemed to have known a better day

and the bards of Ossianic song. When the blind Irish harpist Patrick Byrne visited Scotland some time later, Hill posed him in minstrel's garb in front of Adamson's camera.

The sketch is crowded with figures. Among the principals are Wallace and Bruce, clad in armour; Tam o' Shanter of course, with his drinking crony Souter Johnnie; and also 'the toil-worn cottar', the paterfamilias from *The Cotter's Saturday Night*, over whose head 'Death shakes his sand-glass'. Glimpsed in the background in the roofless kirk at Alloway, the skimpily clad Cutty Sark dances bare-legged with her ghostly partners. A pegleg veteran, son of Mars in *The Jolly Beggars*, keeps watch, while an eye-catching milkmaid poses artfully close by the slumbering poet.

The Kirk is to the fore, represented by a 'ruling elder' and a minister, the latter in long black coat, tile hat and Geneva bands. He clutches a large pulpit Bible. The elder, in tartan bonnet, slyly eyes up Hill's 'several rustic beauties'.

This eclectic assortment of characters also includes a gallimaufry of 'elves, spunkies, brownies, kelpies, etc.' from the land of faerie, and a rather more malign 'crew', as Hill described them, of witches, warlocks and worricows (hobgoblins). Hill depicts them merely as creatures of fantasy – though it may be recalled that, as late as his day, many people, particularly country folk, were half-inclined to believe in the existence of fairies, brownies, bogles and their kind, benign or malevolent.

At the dark end of this spectrum were witches and witchcraft, still strong in folk memory and a potent element in the Scottish psyche. Hugh Miller, in his last terrors, had visions of being hounded by malignant supernaturals. 'Last night,' he said, in the week before he died, 'I felt as if I had been ridden by a witch for fifty miles.' A figment of his tormented imagination? 'It was no dream', he told his doctor.

Somewhat in the background of Hill's phantasmagoric sketch, we see a curious, black-faced, impish figure, ready to give an eldritch skirl on the bagpipes – the devil, no less. It's no surprise to find the great enemy of mankind in such a guise. Mockery and black humour traditionally helped the timid to come to terms with the unthinkably evil, hence the store of colloquial euphemisms for the evil one: Auld Nick, Clootie (for cloven-hoofed), Hornie. Burns, of course, had a good line in fraternising with the enemy, addressing the de'il with finger-wagging familiarity:

> Hear me, auld Hangie, for a wee,
> An' let poor damnéd bodies be …

Even the Scots word 'deil' sounds homelier than the anglicised 'devil'. Hill's sooty imp whose grinning face peers round a pillar at Lincluden Abbey is a far cry from, for example, the sinister long-snouted beast in Dürer's *Knight, Death and Devil*.

But, for Calvinist theologians and for countless of their adherents, the devil was a reality not to be joked about. Satan ruled in hell, on the dark side of the spiritual universe, and hellfire preachers invoked his dire presence. Burns satirised such preachers mercilessly: in his *Holy Fair*, 'Black John' Russel, for one, was singled out for particular scorn. Russel, at that time a minister in Kilmarnock, later went to Cromarty, where Hugh Miller found him equally unpalatable.

> His talk o' Hell, whare devils dwell,
> Our verra 'Sauls does harrow'
> Wi' fright that day.

Even Chalmers, whose stance was more equivocal, could introduce a whiff of brimstone on occasion. 'It makes one shudder', he warned his congregation, 'seriously to think that there may be some here present whom this devouring torrent of wrath shall sweep away; some here present who will be drawn into the whirl of destruction, and forced to take their descending way through the mouth of that pit where the worm dieth not, and the fire is not quenched.'

More potent than Satan, of course, was the just God of the devout. Chalmers and his fellow Evangelicals felt close to the Almighty, believing that they had a direct line to Him in their prayers. They talked to Him. In the words of the 120th metrical psalm:

> In my distress to God I cry'd,
> And he gave ear to me …

David Welsh, when troubled as a youthful parish minister, confided in the Lord through the medium of his diary:

> Oh, I am backward in spiritual things. O Lord, shed abroad Thy love in my heart, by Thy Holy Spirit, for Christ's sake. Amen and Amen. Enable me to cultivate simplicity and godly sincerity. I feel much attachment to my people, but little, little anxiety for their eternal souls. Enable me to be more zealous in this respect ... Lord, what would'st Thou have me to do?

What picture of God had Welsh in his mind when he opened his heart to Him? The more philosophical divines, the learned doctors and professors, as Welsh would become, may have been able to intellectualise, to envisage some disembodied presence that was both personal and otherworldly, but what did the ordinary, unsophisticated worshipper in the pew have in mind when he or she prayed to God? William Blake, the visionary artist–poet, had clothed his figures of God and the Son in plain ankle-length smocks. Perhaps they would picture him like that. If not, then perhaps a being blurred in the mists of eternity, all-seeing, all-knowing, and yet somehow real and tangible in the here and now, and never so close as in Presbyterian Scotland in the 1840s.

Unlike Episcopalians and Roman Catholics, the Scots Presbyterians of the time had no truck with images. The church where the Disruption Assembly met, St Andrew's and St George's as it has become, has stained-glass windows now, but in 1843 the panes were clear. If David Octavius Hill had been painting in another tradition, he might have found a place for God in an upper corner, if not in the dead centre of his canvas. But this was a plain-clothed, top-hatted and bonneted, seemly assembly, and God was not expected in person.

All the same, Hill was conscious of God's presence in Tanfield Hall that day in May. God is not in the picture – unless, metaphorically, in the ray of sunlight slanting down from the skylight on the heads of Thomas Chalmers and Patrick MacFarlan, and on the deed being signed on the table.

14

The king is dead

A small oil painting of *Dr Chalmers and his Grandson* attracted attention when exhibited by the Royal Scottish Academy. It showed the ageing Chalmers on a rustic seat with his grandson Thomas Chalmers Hanna leaning on his knee. Chalmers holds his stick in one hand and clasps the boy affectionately round the waist with the other. Sunlight filters through shady trees, striking his domed forehead and casting one side of his face into deep shadow – but also highlighting a butterfly poised on the arm of the bench. A small archway affords a glimpse into a corner of sunlit garden beyond, as if beckoning to a secret place.

The painting is by David Octavius Hill. It can be seen today at the Scottish National Portrait Gallery, although it's hung too high on the wall for the details to be seen clearly.

In *Dr Chalmers and his Grandson*, the artist followed a Hill and Adamson calotype more closely than in any other of his paintings. The subject is almost identical. Some details have been altered or tidied: in the calotype, the boy's head is blurred and the grandfather's eyes are hidden in deep shade. They emerge in the painting. The bare setting of the calotype, in which only the two figures, the bench and the hint of a doorway at the back can be seen, is transformed in the painting into a romantic idyll, man and boy embowered in a sun-dappled grove.

And perhaps Hill has introduced a suggestion of passing time and mortality. The butterfly – does it hint at the transitoriness of life? And the sundial with a scythe propped against it, just visible in the half-revealed garden? When Hill painted the scene, Chalmers had been dead barely a year. It was the artist's posthumous tribute to a man he admired.

The end came without warning. In the spring of 1847, four years after the Disruption, Chalmers returned home from an extended visit to London. While there, he was called to give evidence to a House of Commons inquiry into the refusal of Scottish lairds to grant sites on their land where Free Kirk members could worship. He also found time to address London audiences from the pulpit, preaching – as the *Witness* recorded – with all his old fire and vehemence at three services which were attended by a number of eminent people, among whom were Lord John Russell, the Whig prime minister, and several leading politicians. Chalmers came home on a Friday night in good spirits, though his colleague Dr William Cunningham, with whom he attended morning service at the Free Church of Morningside that Sunday, reflected with the benefit of hindsight that he had detected an intangible change in his demeanour – 'his temper and talk seemed more of one already translated than of one still walking on earth'.

That night, Chalmers went to bed well enough and meaning to rise early, as he had a report to deliver to the General Assembly, which was in session at the time. At six o'clock in the morning when he should have rung his bell, as his custom was, for a cup of coffee, the bell was silent. At twenty to eight, his next-door neighbour Patrick Macdougall, formerly professor of moral philosophy at Edinburgh University and now at the Free Church college, sent round to inquire if a packet of papers had been left out for him; he and Chalmers had talked the previous day, and he had expected them to be delivered. Chalmers' housekeeper knocked at the bedroom door but got no reply. Assuming he was still sleeping, she told the messenger the packet would be sent over as soon as he wakened. Half an hour later, there was another caller for the doctor – there was early business afoot – and again the housekeeper failed to get a response. Now she summoned the other servants – a comfortable household in Morningside would have several – to a conference at the bedroom door. Hesitantly pushing the door open, they entered to find the doctor half-sitting in bed on his pillows. His arms were folded on his chest, and his face was peaceful, but there was no sign of life.

What to do? They put their heads together, decided not to tell the family for the time being, and, instead, sent word to Macdougall. The professor rushed over, burst into the room and drew back the curtains round the bed. He took the doctor's hand; it was, as he said, cold as marble. It was thought he had been dead for several hours, and perhaps he had not even settled down for sleep when the blow struck. Papers, pen and ink were beside his bed ready for work when he awoke; his watch was under his pillow. His face was serene. It was as if – as the *Witness* put it – he was telling them: 'I am gone up'.

The news of Chalmers' death was announced to a hushed Free Kirk Assembly when proceedings were opened that day at noon. Some of them wept. It was felt that the day's business should be postponed; and, after a solemn service of worship had been held, the session was closed. 'The whole Christian world will deplore this loss', declared the *Witness* leader-writer, presumably Miller. 'It is the foremost champion of Christianity who has fallen.' Members of the Auld Kirk were meeting in their Assembly at the same time, but the death of Chalmers went unrecorded there.

Mr Alex Hill (brother of David Octavius), printseller in ordinary to Her Majesty, was quick to capitalise on the sad event. In a press advertisement, he respectfully called attention to a sale of engravings of Dr Chalmers lately made from the portrait by Thomas Duncan, which were to be had in the form of proof, print, or in a handsome rosewood frame from his gallery at 67 Princes Street. 'A very small number of the Choice Autograph Proofs remain unsold', he announced; and, to prevent disappointment, early application was recommended 'by all who would wish to possess' such an engraving 'in its perfect state'.

Several complimentary quotations from the press were offered as further recommendation, including this from the *Weekly Journal*: 'It presents him as he is, with the traces of the wasting studies of years on his homely but remarkable features, and they are lighted up with the fire of genius, and softened by the glow of benevolence, so as at once to give a living likeness of this great and good man'.

The funeral was impressive, though the day was cheerless: 'one of those days which steep the landscape in a sombre neutral tint of gray – a sort of diluted gloom, and volumes of mist, unvariegated, blank, and diffuse of outline, flew low athwart the hills, or lay folded on the distant horizon. A chill breeze from the east murmured drearily through the trees.' However, it was felt that garish sunshine would have suited the occasion ill.

One estimate put the crowds at 100,000. The coffin was followed by 200 people in a two-mile circuitous route to the grave in the new Grange cemetery, south of the Meadows, not far from the Chalmers home in Morningside. Though Chalmers had selected this resting place beforehand, some felt a little cheated. 'We had at one time half wished that Chalmers should have been buried in the Greyfriars', wrote Miller, recalling that it was there that the Covenant had been signed 'and where the dust of so many of the martyrs lie'. But Grange was 'a singularly beautiful spot', surrounded as it then was by green fields, and commanding a prospect of every striking feature of the city and its neighbourhood – the 'purple Pentlands' and Arthur's Seat 'just at the point of view where the lion-like contour of the eminence is most complete'.

Shops closed as the cortege approached. Forty carriages were counted going by, not including those of relatives and close friends. Four horses with their grooms drew the hearse, which was followed by two mutes. The fathers and brethren from the Assembly came out in force, but the prevailing black of the mourners was leavened by a splash of civic colour, as the city magistrates joined the column dressed in their scarlet cloaks.

Miller reported on the funeral in the *Witness* in the manner which the occasion demanded. 'There was a moral sublimity in the spectacle. It was the dust of a Presbyterian minister which the coffin contained; and yet they were burying him amid the tears of a nation, and with more than kingly honours.' Cockburn commented, with more restraint: 'I doubt if there was ever such a funeral of a private individual in Scotland'.

Truly, Chalmers had been kingly. Yet, by the time of his death, he was already distanced from the centre of influence. He remains a key figure in Hill's picture, but Hill has shifted him from the focus of attention. If Chalmers had been king, heirs–apparent were at his elbow jockeying to take his place. Younger and more aggressive men were putting their stamp on the church he had led – not into the wilderness, to be sure, though it must have seemed like that to roofless congregations in remoter parishes, but into an unknown and uncertain future.

There was big William Cunningham, pugnacious and polemical – not a learned man, unlike his fellow reverend doctors, his only degree an honorary doctorate from Princeton, New Jersey. He was an out-and-out Calvinist: good deeds alone would not get you to heaven – read the Bible – beware the wrath of God! A disappointment in the pulpit, he was a fierce debater, notorious for using 'such severity of language as led many to form an unfavourable view of his character'. But friends rallied round to declare he was gentle at heart despite the rough words. He followed Chalmers as professor of church history at the new Free Church college, but did not quite fill his shoes; he was a narrower man.

And there was Robert Smith Candlish, the young minister of St George's, Edinburgh, at the time of the Disruption – 'destined to become the foremost ecclesiastic of the post-Disruption Church', according to a present-day Free Kirk leader. Candlish, small in stature and thrusting by nature, was a firebrand preacher and ardent Calvinist interpreter of Biblical texts. His *Exposition of the Book of Genesis* was published in 1843. He would become, in due course, principal of the Free Kirk college and professor of apologetics – apologetics meaning 'the argumentative defence of Christianity'. To him, the 'free' in Free Church meant freedom from all ties with the state, in opposition to the Chalmers ideal of church establishment; and it was the Candlish view that prevailed.

Somewhere in the background, there was a family link with the poet Burns, who described Candlish senior as 'the earliest friend except my brother, whom I have on earth'. Candlish's mother Jane was one of the *Belles of Mauchline* in the poem of that name – 'Miss Smith she has wit'.

Candlish had no formal schooling; his father died when he was five weeks old, and he was taught at home by his mother and his elder brother and sister before attending Glasgow University, after which he tutored at Eton. He leapt to prominence with an eloquent speech from the back benches at the 1839 assembly, after which his place in the hierarchy was assured. It was he who proposed suspending the Strathbogie Seven, an inflammatory decision which racked up the tension in the Kirk's increasingly bitter conflict with the Court of Session. When he was offered the new chair of Biblical criticism at Edinburgh University by the then home secretary, his nomination roused such indignation, vehemently expressed in the House of Lords by Lord Aberdeen, that it was withdrawn.

Candlish could be a formidable antagonist; a letter-writer to the *Scotsman* newspaper described him in 1843 as the autocrat of the Evangelical party. Jaw stuck out, he looks the young Turk in the photographs. Hill gave him a prominent position in the picture and, just possibly, toyed with the idea of making him the key figure. One of his early sketches shows a Candlish lookalike addressing the Assembly.

Though Candlish had energetically pushed for Hugh Miller to be editor of the *Witness*, he underwent a change of heart soon after the Disruption. Candlish thought the paper should be the Kirk's official mouthpiece, but Miller would have none of it and increasingly took his own independent line. What happened is not entirely clear – muddied, perhaps, by the fact that our authority is not impartial, being Miller himself. Candlish, seeking to curb Miller's editorial independence, circulated a paper critical of him and proposing to put the paper in the hands of a Kirk committee. Miller got wind of this whispering campaign, obtained a copy of the paper and fired off his own pugnacious riposte in which he warned against censorship and accused Candlish of being the censor-in-chief. Chalmers intervened shortly before his death, knocking heads together on Miller's behalf. 'Which of you could direct Hugh Miller?' he asked scornfully – and, possibly, affectionately. As a result, Candlish was bested and Miller stayed in the editor's chair.

The Free Kirk, in a worldly sense, went from strength to strength. With Chalmers at the helm, the 1843 Assembly members set themselves a daunting task, 'nothing less than that of producing a complete and exact replica for the Establishment they had left', as a present-day church historian put it. 'In every parish a Free Church should stand over against the old parish church, manse over against manse, Free Church school over against the old parochial school.' They set up a college – in the end, three colleges – to train their students for the ministry. 'Chalmers, sanguine as always, had absolute confidence that the money required would be forthcoming whether in large contributions from the wealthy or in small ones from humbler folk' – the widow's mite replicated a thousandfold.

'His expectations were not completely realized, but his appeal met with astonishing success.' The writer of these words, J. H. S. Burleigh, in *A Church History of Scotland*, contended that nothing comparable had happened in Scotland since the days of King David I, the 'sair sanct'. He was the twelfth-century founder of numerous monasteries and abbeys, Holyrood among them. It was not possible for such giving to have taken place before the industrial revolution brought wealth to the middle classes. 'Satanic mills' as the new industrial factories were known, provided the wherewithal to build new temples to the glory of God.

Chalmers himself devised what was called the sustention fund to compensate ministers for the stipends they had lost on leaving the establishment. Contributions from each congregation, according to a scale of what they could afford, allowed ministers to be paid an 'equal dividend', which wealthier congregations might top up to give their own incumbents more. It had been calculated that a penny a week from each church member would produce a stipend of £150 a year for 500 ministers. It ensured that the pastors who gave up their all did not starve.

Nor did the parish schoolteachers who had lost their jobs (since education was a function of the parish system) when they joined the Disruption. A network of Free Church schools was set up throughout the country under the control of Robert Candlish, who ensured that they remained strictly for Free Church children. Chalmers in the last days of his life demurred at this exclusivity. So did Guthrie, father of the Ragged School movement, and Hugh Miller; but they were in the minority.

There was an amazing boom in church-building. Within a year of the Disruption, nearly 500 new churches had been built, usually of a plain and unostentatious kind, and often standing cheek by jowl with the auld skyward-pointing kirks. This simplified the transfer of allegiance from one side of the street to the other. By the fourth year from the Disruption, the total number of free kirks had risen to 700, hence the abundance of redundant church buildings today.

Chalmers might have seen all this as a hollow victory. He had led his followers out of the establishment in 1843 convinced that the Auld Kirk was moribund, its leadership sterile, and that its people would desert en masse for the Kirk he led. In that scenario, the government would be forced to come to an accommodation and offer the Free Kirk some form of establishment. The Free Kirk was, in his eyes, the true and legitimate Church of Scotland, and it should be recognised as such.

But he misinterpreted the signs. Outmanoeuvred by the government and the courts, the Evangelicals had lost their ten-year dominance in the Assembly. The walkout of 1843, exhilarating though it was, left the Moderates in a seeming majority clinging to power. It was not they who had left the fold. Meantime, the Free Kirk developed a dynamic of its own, led by energetic radicals like Candlish and Cunningham who rejected any form of establishment and frankly rejoiced in having cut the last ties with the state. Headstrong young Turks set the pace. Chalmers would have been appalled. The very success of the Free Kirk killed any lingering hope of healing the rift, even when patronage – the rock on which the Kirk had split – was abolished later in the century. Reconciliation did not come for many years after that.

It's possible to see Chalmers by the time of the Disruption as sidelined, a figurehead rather than a leader. Recently, a writer asserted that 'the story of Chalmers' life is in the last analysis the story of failure'. It seems a harsh judgement. But what had he achieved? By lending his prestige to a course which led inevitably to secession, he ended up dealing a massive blow to the cause he loved. He desired to free the Established Church from the reins of the state; but instead, the Disruption brought about disunity. A weakened Auld Kirk retained the benefits of establishment, and the Free Kirk took a route he had not envisaged.

As for the social experiment he instigated at St John's in Glasgow, based on his ideal of a Christian community, its apparent success proved transitory. Chalmers had hoped to purify society and, in doing so, to rescue the huddled masses from their abject poverty. The plan had not worked.

But failure? Looking at Hill's portrait of him and his grandson, painted after his death, you may fancy you see failure in his eyes: here's a sad old man, work done, reflecting on mortality. But that's to read more into it than it will bear. You analyse the picture, not the man. *Dr Chalmers and his Grandson* is the image of a man and boy done in oils, derived from a salted photographic print, which was formed on treated paper as the result of some minutes' exposure to the light in an Edinburgh garden one sunny day. No more. It tells nothing of the intellect, the strength of character, the fiery eloquence, the commanding presence – of the spirit or the soul. Failure was not in the minds of the many thousands, of whatever faith, who stood silent as he was carried to the grave.

15

A shot in the dark

In a room of paintings from the Victorian era in the Scottish National Portrait Gallery in Edinburgh, there are several portraits of people who figure in this story. Here you will find two heroes and one villain of the Disruption, plus some neutrals. There is one notable absentee.

Thomas Chalmers appears twice. There is the *Dr Chalmers and his Grandson* described in the previous chapter. He is also shown three-quarter-length in a painting by Thomas Duncan, looking out of the canvas with hooded dreamy-grey eyes, with one hand on his Bible and the other holding a quill pen. There is a small painting by James Edgar of *Dr Guthrie on a Mission of Mercy* in which a portly Thomas Guthrie in top hat stands in the Lawnmarket with the church of St Giles in the background. Guthrie, a founder of 'ragged schools' for street children, has a hand on the head of an urchin. More children surround him, and a woman with a pitcher watches from her seat on a stone step. This Guthrie is older than the man pictured in Hill and Adamson's calotype, where he appears tall and slim and quite elegant.

Lord Brougham, the arch enemy and target of Hugh Miller's wrath, has a commanding position. A large canvas by Andrew Morton shows him seated, dressed all in black, up to his cravat and down to his spats. His gaze is cool.

Artists – being a self-perpetuating race in paint – are represented by Thomas Duncan, painted by Robert Scott Lauder, and Sir George Harvey by John Ballantyne. This is an elderly Harvey, rather squat in the figure, standing at his easel in a garret – a spacious one. In a corner on the floor are some of his props as a painter of historical scenes – a basket-hilted sword, a plaid and a brass-bound volume which may be a Bible.

Finally there is John Wilson, alias 'Christopher North' of *Blackwood's Magazine*, in another portrait by Thomas Duncan. A friend described Wilson, breathlessly, as 'a true upright, knocking-down, poetical, prosaic, moral, professional, hard-drinking, fierce-eating, good-looking, honourable and straightforward Tory' – so he was presumably no great fan of the Evangelical set. He affects a flaring red waistcoat and shirt open at the chest, with flowing ginger locks, and striking a pose in a fake outdoors with his hand on the muzzle of a sporting gun.

And Hugh Miller? Is that him with the plaid draped round his shoulders, clutching his staff? At first glance, maybe – but no, it's the poetical shepherd James Hogg. Hugh Miller finds no place in the Edinburgh pantheon. In fact, so far as is known, no portrait in oils of him exists – and this is an oddity considering his status in the cultural Scotland of the nineteenth century. True, there are busts, including those sculpted by his second wife, and there are the marvellous Hill and Adamson calotypes as well as later photographs. One of the latter shows him serge-suited – no longer the bare-armed working mason – with top hat upturned on the table and a hand lens held to his eye, inspecting one of his geological samples, a fossil maybe. This is Miller gentrified.

Yet the absent Miller had perhaps more celebrity status than any. His figure in its prominent position at the forefront of Hill's Disruption painting would be instantly recognisable to all who saw it. Miller was more widely known even than the majestic Thomas Chalmers. His first book, *The Old Red Sandstone*, was a runaway scientific, literary and popular success 'on a scale barely surpassed by *Uncle Tom's Cabin*', in the words of Lynn Barber in her *The Heyday of Natural History*, and his name became 'known in every Victorian parlour'. The works that followed in quick succession were bestsellers. Maybe he was just too busy to sit for a formal portrait.

Barber wrote that 'Miller bravely faced the dangers that other writers shunned, and led his readers to safety through the thickets of geological controversy, with a fossil fish in one hand and the Book of Genesis in the other … Even fundamentalists found that they could read Miller's geological expositions without hearing any distant crackling from the flames of hell-fire.'

His last work on that subject was published posthumously. The *Testimony of the Rocks* was his definitive attempt to reconcile scientific discovery with his belief in God the creator.

Miller was born in 1802, which makes him an exact contemporary of David Octavius Hill, in the small but thriving east-coast port of Cromarty, north of Inverness. His mother Harriet was a tall, slim girl of eighteen when he was born. Miller was five when his father, skipper of a trading sloop that plied the Scottish coasts, drowned when the vessel foundered in a gale. He grew up an adventurous, self-willed, rebellious boy, a trial to his mother. She was stricken with grief when her two daughters, younger than Hugh, were struck down with fever, dying within days of each other at the ages of eleven and nine. The boy, not yet fifteen, witnessed her heartbreak and flinched when he heard her cry shame on God for taking a daughter and not the son.

He got into scrapes, sometimes with the younger John Swanson, who became a friend for life. Once, they were trapped by the sea while exploring caves on the shore. Another escapade proved even more dangerous. Swanson's father, like Miller's, captained a trading smack, which was armed with a few twelve-pounder guns during the Napoleonic wars. The boys carried away a bag of gunpowder and had fun making miniature volcanoes in the Swanson garden. That night, Swanson took the remains of the gunpowder to the garret where he slept, and made the mistake of gloating over it with a lighted candle in his hand. The explosion blinded him for days, and his parents blamed the tearaway Miller for leading him astray.

Miller quit formal schooling after a fist-fight in the classroom with the teacher. He learned the stonemason's trade in the quarries of Easter Ross near his home, then followed the trade on the west coast and on an extended visit to Edinburgh. But the stone dust affected his lungs, and he returned to Cromarty to recover his health.

There he renewed his friendship with Swanson, who was by then running a grocer's shop in the town – which he soon forsook to study the ministry in Aberdeen. Swanson was already a zealot, while Miller at that stage was a sceptic – Bible stories were little more than fables; but his friend was persuasive. 'I pant after the time when I may be fully assured that you are travelling towards Zion', he wrote from Aberdeen. Miller, with time on his hands, read widely, thought deeply and took the first steps on the way.

He also turned his mason's hand to literature, without success. His *Poems Written in the Leisure Hours of a Journeyman Mason* (publication by the *Inverness Courier* paid for out of his own pocket) was coolly received. 'We are glad to understand that our author has the good sense to rely more on his chisel than the Muses', a critic wrote. The volume brought him not fame or fortune but an invitation to contribute to the *Courier*. The resulting series of articles on herring-fishing in Cromarty showed him fully fledged as a descriptive writer. It was immediately successful – and even more so when republished as a pamphlet. Miller's biographer, George Rosie, says that 'it had Sir Walter Scott scrambling for a copy after the run was exhausted'. Miller was getting known; he had his foot on the ladder.

Miller, it seemed, was not the marrying type. His 'bachelor wife' was a creation of fancy, an imaginary companion with whom he conversed on his solitary walks. However, close to the Miller home in Cromarty there lived a widow, Elizabeth Fraser, whose eighteen-year-old daughter, Lydia, joined her there after schooling in Edinburgh and a spell with relatives in Surrey. Lydia was a lively, intelligent and good-looking girl. 'Her portrait', writes Elizabeth Sutherland, her biographer, 'shows her to have been small, pretty and vivacious with dark hair arranged in the fashion of the day with a knot at the back of the head and corkscrew ringlets either side of an oval face.' 'I don't know how or why it was that I never met the Cromarty Poet, as he was called', Lydia wrote in her journal. 'Our spheres lay quite apart. I'm afraid I loved as much gaiety as I could get while he lived in his old contemplative philosophic ideal.'

But not so old philosophic. They *did* meet, a few times, at 'the charming tea-parties of the place', as he called them, and once she observed him on a visit to a charity school. 'I was greatly struck by the thoughtful look of his countenance, especially the eye … The chiselling was fine, the colouring a deep-blue tinged with sapphire … But what struck me most was its earnest and deeply pensive cast.'

A chance meeting – in the romantic surroundings of an ancient chapel – one summer Sunday evening set the seal on their developing relationship. They spoke briefly, but it was enough: 'I knelt at a cold gravestone and registered over the dead a vow, rash and foolish perhaps, but it was kept'. The widow Fraser at first disapproved, wanting better for her daughter than a working stonemason. But she softened in time; and, when the banker Robert Paul offered Miller a job and he put away his mason's tools, she relented. Lydia and her Hugh married in 1837.

When Miller took up mallet and chisel for the last time two years later, it was with a heavy heart. They'd had a daughter, Eliza – 'a delight and wonder to Hugh above all wonders. Her little smiles and caresses sent him always away to his daily toil with a lighter heart.' But Eliza fell ill, and, after a time, she died. She smiled no more. He carved her headstone in St Regulus churchyard – the place where Lydia had spoken her secret 'rash and foolish' vow to marry him.

Miller's interest in geology stemmed from his boyhood rambles along the shoreline near his home. 'The shores of Cromarty are strewed over with water-rolled fragments of primary rocks,' he wrote in *My Schools and Schoolmasters*, 'and I soon learned to take a deep interest in sauntering over the various pebble-beds when shaken up by recent storms, and in learning to distinguish their numerous components.' Once he had found an old hammer with a black oak shaft and a square compact head, he went about 'breaking into all manner of stones, with great perseverance and success'. He was delighted with what the hammer blows revealed.

'I found, in a large-grained granite, a few sheets of beautiful black mica, that, when split exceedingly thin, and pasted between slips of mica of the ordinary kind, made admirably-coloured eye-glasses, that converted the landscapes around into richly-toned drawings of sepia.' Rich sepia drawings – it sounds like a description of the calotype photographs he would later see in the Hill and Adamson studio.

Gradually, as he learned more, he passed from mineralogy to geology. His apprenticeship in the quarries of the Black Isle gave him a familiarity with rock strata, though it seems he found no fossils there. That came later. He read books and scoured the cliffs and seashore in search of the petrified life-forms embedded in stone. His great find came in 1830 when a lucky strike brought evidence of his first fossil fish to light. He pieced his fossil fragments together and identified ancient fish that no-one had seen or suspected before. He wondered at the age of the earth when these creatures were created, lived, died and turned to stone, extinct, a long time ago, before Adam. He pondered God's creation.

The Old Red Sandstone first appeared as a series of articles that Miller wrote to fill space in the *Witness* in the dog days of summer 1840. By chance, they came to the notice of Roderick Murchison, president of the Geological Society. Murchison, an indefatigable cracker of stones across the continent, a former fox-hunting man who moved in the best of society and whose unstoppable upward progress would be crowned with a baronetcy, was astonished by the discoveries made by this rough-hewn plebeian and delighted by the vigour with which he described them. They met, and Murchison persuaded Miller to publish the series in book form.

He then took steps to bring Miller to wider attention, as few, more likely none, of his scientific peers would be subscribers to the *Witness*. At the meeting of the Royal Association for the Advancement of Science, held that year in Glasgow, Murchison 'spoke in the highest terms of Mr Miller's perseverance and ingenuity as a geologist'. Miller the self-educated man had managed 'to elevate himself to a position which any man in any sphere of life might well envy'. Furthermore, his papers on geology were 'written in a style so beautiful and poetical, as to throw plain geologists like himself into the shade'. The learned audience cheered. William Buckland, who combined enthusiasm for geology and theology in his own person – he was dean of Westminster – was equally smitten, saying he would give his left hand to possess such descriptive powers.

As proof of Miller's standing in the geological world, the eminent Swiss-born but America-based Louis Agassiz proposed to the Royal Association that the strange carapaced winged fish that Miller had discovered in beds of old red sandstone sometime in the early 1830s should be named after its finder. *Pterichthyodes milleri* was born. Agassiz may have visited Miller in Cromarty, but certainly they both took part in a meeting of geologists at the home of the Gordon-Cummings family at Altyre, near Forres. Murchison and Buckland were also among the party, and all muddied themselves scrambling among the fossil-bearing rocks along the Findhorn river.

Geology had overturned a contemporary theory that the earth was a mere 6,000 years old. The new science indicated a much vaster time-scale. In the eighteenth century, the Scottish geologist James Hutton had found 'no vestige of a beginning' in the history of the earth, and − what may have been just as offensive to the Evangelical mind − 'no prospect of an end'. More disturbing to those who believed in the absolute authority of the Bible were certain other questions. How could the Biblical story of the creation be sustained in the face of evidence that showed a long, slow progression rather than a six-day burst of divine energy? Furthermore, why had it taken uncountable millions of years before God breathed life into Adam and Eve? Why had scaly sea forms, such as Miller had found on an Orkney shore, been given priority? Most unsettling of all was the suggestion that all life-forms, including human beings made in the image of God, had developed their present forms in a long evolutionary process. Why hadn't the all-wise Creator got it right first time?

Darwin had yet to publish, but his precursors were already pointing the way. The appearance in the 1840s of a book called *The Vestiges of Creation*, which uncannily prefigured some of Darwin's theories, raised a storm of controversy throughout Britain. Miller mounted an attack on it in his *Footprints of the Creator*. Had he learned that the anonymous author was the Edinburgh journalist and publisher Robert Chambers, a man whom he admired, he would have been appalled.

Miller was a believer and a Calvinist. Unlike the rationalists, the sceptics, the radical atheists who seized on the findings of geology to undermine faith in a divinely ordered creation, he believed profoundly in an almighty if unknowable and unpredictable God. He had absolute faith in the authority of the Bible, and he managed to square its inconsistencies to his own satisfaction. 'Between the Word and the Works of God there can be no actual discrepancies', he wrote. The six days of Genesis were fact, but not necessarily consecutive. Miller proposed a series of distinct creations aeons apart, in each of which new species sprang fully formed in their perfection and then, over time, slowly degenerated. Creation was a renewable phenomenon.

It has been argued that increasing doubts undermining his long-held and deeply felt religious beliefs overset his mind. This doesn't seem likely. He marshalled his arguments as forcefully as ever in *Testimony*. And he was spared the worst. He died three years before Darwin unleashed his *On the Origin of Species*.

Miller went to bed troubled on the night of 23 December 1856. For some time past, he had been plagued by strange delusions, irrational fears, terrible dreams, terrors in the night. He felt, literally, that he was hag-ridden – 'ridden by a witch for fifty miles', he told his doctor. Sometime during the night he rose, pulled on a big jersey, and took up the revolver he kept by his bedside. Next morning, a servant found him lying dead at his bedroom door with a bullet wound in his chest. The ball had skimmed his heart and cut an artery.

The *Witness*, in an edition rushed out that morning, alleged an accident. It speculated that Miller, wakened by a nightmare and hearing sounds he took to be someone breaking into the geological museum which he kept at his home in Portobello, had seized the weapon and dashed for the door, perhaps tripping in his haste, and the gun had gone off. But there was the matter of a note in his handwriting addressed to his wife:

'My brain burns. God and father of the Lord Jesus, have mercy upon me. Dearest Lydia, dear children, farewell.'

So it was no accident; it was suicide. He had put the muzzle to his chest and pulled the trigger. This was hard for his sympathisers to take. Suicide carried a deep stigma in the Victorian mind, being the recourse of criminals, people wildly disturbed, godless miscreants: 'It looked rum in a leading spokesman for the Free Church' is the pithy comment of a modern writer.

Dr William Hanna, who was not a medical man but a minister, the son-in-law and biographer of Thomas Chalmers and a friend of Miller, rushed into print with the information that 'for some months past his overtasked intellect had given evidence of disorder'. Only two days before his death, Hanna reported, Miller had gone to his physician having convinced himself that his brain was 'giving way': 'I cannot put two thoughts together today', he said. The same physician and three others had no doubt, in determining the cause of death, that the fatal act was 'suicidal under the impulse of insanity'. Poor Miller had gone mad. Since he had been at least temporarily out of his mind, the proprieties could be observed and he could be given a Christian burial. And so he was, and it was remarked that the crowds attending his funeral were almost as large as those at Chalmers'.

Whether Miller was deranged is a moot point, not verifiable now. He had exhibited eccentricities and was the prey of fearful obsessions. The revolver was not the only loaded firearm kept to hand, and sometimes, even, presented in the street. He had a pathological fear of break-ins. He had trouble sleeping, and, when he did, suffered from distressing dreams. Whatever troubled him, the only known fact is that he turned the gun on himself.

16

So many *kent* faces

Amelia Paton was plain, plump and in her forties when she married David Octavius Hill. He was sixty. She was an artist, and sister of an artist, Joseph Noel Paton. She had studied in Rome, and most likely first met Hill in 1844, three years after the death of his first wife, Ann, when two of her works were hung in the Royal Scottish Academy exhibition.

She became best known as a sculptor, her subjects for busts including her husband – there's one on his grave at Dean cemetery and another in the Edinburgh portrait gallery – and Thomas Carlyle. Her statue of the missionary explorer David Livingstone stands in Princes Street Gardens, and her statue of Robert Burns, cut in marble – inexpertly, it was claimed – by quarry craftsmen from the model she sent to Italy, is in Dumfries. She was commissioned to sculpt some of the statuary in the niches of the Scott monument in Edinburgh. After D. O.'s death she became rich, not by artistic endeavour but because of her friendship with the millionaire industrialist and benefactor Andrew Carnegie. Some of the gilt rubbed off. He advised her on investments and they paid off.

Hill was still labouring at it in August 1860 when he wrote to his friend the painter David Roberts in London: 'I have brought out my big figure Picture here [to Grange House, south of Edinburgh] desiring to dedicate the summer in pushing it on towards completion rather than sketching. There is a great deal of gin-horse work to be gone through before the end is in sight.' There's no way of knowing what stage he had reached by then, or what progress he made at Grange. Two years later, writing to his sister Jane to tell her that he was to marry Amelia, he confided that 'she is resolved that the Picture shall be done!'

As Mrs Hill, Amelia's efforts were not confined to inspiring, cajoling and wheedling, or to the wifely duties of making sure he had hot dinners. Possibly the painting would have remained unfinished but for her. She took up the brush herself as his eager assistant, though we can only guess the extent of her contribution. Reminiscing years later, she told an interviewer: 'I well remember Dr Candlish, when he paid us the wedding call, placing his hands on my shoulders and saying – *Now we look to you to see that your husband's picture of the Disruption is speedily completed.* I used often to work at it in the early morning before D. O. was about' – surreptitiously at first – 'putting in the shirt fronts and collars.' Hill knew what she was up to: 'You need not think that your work has been unobserved by me', he told her. 'But go on.' Then, growing more adventurous, she worked at the faces. But how many faces, and whose? – that she didn't say.

News of progress leaked out in June 1864 when the *Scotsman* carried a brief but accurate description. The writer must have had a good look at it, taken on a guided tour round the canvas by the artist, perhaps. Certain details caught his eye: the 'trim, courtly features of the father of Mrs Beecher Stowe', the 'inimitable rendering of the Oriental lineaments, tawny eyes and lithe grace of the Parsee convert', and 'the thin floating hair of the great preacher [Chalmers] so managed that it forms almost a halo round his head' (an un-Presbyterian fancy). By then the end was in sight, and the *Scotsman* raised the question of where the finished work should go: 'Surely there is but one place for this picture and that is the National Gallery. The members of the Free Church will no doubt exert themselves to obtain it for their hall, but few would see it there, and none would see it well.'

The official unveiling came in May 1866. After the private view attended by Hill's friends and fellow artists, a paragraph in the press announced that Mr D. O. Hill's picture 'in which are upwards of four hundred portraits' could now be seen at the Calton Convening Rooms in Waterloo Place, a stone's throw from Rock House. It could be viewed from nine o'clock in the morning until five in the evening. Admission cost a shilling with a concession of sixpence for young persons under fourteen years. Ministers of the Free Church and their families got in free, likewise clergymen of all other denominations on presentation of their cards or writing their names in the visitors' book. Since the Kirk Assemblies were sitting, the show was nicely timed to draw the maximum number of interested clerics. Quite a few would be eager to scour the canvas in search of themselves.

'It is alive and arrests', a journalist enthused. 'You feel as well as see the crowd of eager faces; and you set about searching among them for your familiars as you would in a real crowd.' It was, after all, only twenty-three years after the event; many of the men and women pictured were still living, and some were still to be seen daily on the streets of Edinburgh and elsewhere and on Sundays in the pulpit.

Some personalities could be recognised at once. So many *kent* faces, as the journalist said; Chalmers for one, 'the prince among his peers' standing lonely and seeming curiously apart amid his seated brethren in the exact midpoint of the canvas; Hugh Miller prominent in the foreground, hunched over his notebook. 'We caught the eye of Cunningham' (William Cunningham, a mighty churchman in his time, whose eye by then had glazed) – 'big, combative, irascible', leaning forward to watch the signing in progress below. The names of some – Chalmers and especially Miller – still resonate; but Cunningham, like so many others, is a forgotten man. By that date, twenty years on, recollection was already beginning to fade.

Above the gathering, several faces can be seen at skylights in the roof, a good vantage point for onlookers. On the right, against a blue sky with a seagull in flight, are three Newhaven fishermen; on the left, another Newhaven man, identifiable as Willie Liston, and, oddly, the elderly John Henning, a sculptor who featured in several Hill and Adamson photographs. You see them in the painting, but it's most unlikely that they were there. And if by chance they were, would they have clambered on to the roof for a better view? It seems doubtful – and unsafe! But there they are; Hill has given them a virtual presence as witnesses at the show.

What do they see below? They see, if they crane their necks, old Dr Somerville approach 'with tottering steps' and stiffened hand 'to add his dying testimony' to the deed on the table. (And we see him, white-headed, quill in hand, and ramrod straight in spite of his frailty.) They see Angus McGillivray 'in extremity of feebleness but with joy of heart', head bowed, supported by his sons as he shuffles forward to sign 'with a dying hand'. He was eighty.

They see John Macdonald, the picture of health, black-haired in spite of his sixty-four years, ruddy-faced, heavy-jowled, big-framed – and able to bellow like a bull by the look of him. He needed to. He was a great revivalist, a preacher to thousands in the open air. In the calotype which Hill and Adamson took of him, his fleshy hand rests on a book. In the painting, he stands at the table, dead centre, below Thomas Chalmers, waiting his turn to sign the deed.

Macdonald was called the Apostle of the North. 'Ten thousand people have often been swayed as one man, stirred into enthusiasm or melted into sadness by this mighty and faithful preacher's voice' – mighty voice indeed to reach the multitude gathered on the hillsides. He spoke in Gaelic, of course. 'From Tarbatness to the outer Hebrides – from the Spey to the Pentland Firth – the fact needed but to be known that John Macdonald had come and was about to preach the word, in order that the country for twenty miles around should gather at his call.'

In his younger days, he was minister at the Gaelic chapel in Edinburgh, and so big a crowd-puller that English-speakers pleaded with him to preach in their native tongue. So he added a third service in English to the two he held in Gaelic. On the day he gave his last in Edinburgh before moving north to Ferintosh, the crowd waiting to hear him was so great that the keys of a bigger church were sent for. Through the Grassmarket he marched on the way to the West Kirk with his congregation at his heels, and when he left there were tears and sobbing.

Alexander Campbell of Monzie combined the sporting and the spiritual in his life. He was a death-dealer on the hillside. Laird, 'free kirkman and purist', he loved to be out on the moors with his gun: 'the St Bartholomew of Grouse', he was called. In August 1846, on the glorious twelfth, he wagered he would down 230 brace 'besides wounding and sending miserably into Eternity three times as many'. A guest reported that he 'gave me a splendid dinner of venison-tripe and full-bosomed grouse, with a magnum of brandy-and-water'. Their talk mingled deer-stalking and good fellowship with pious scraps of gospel and revival hymns. 'He and I got on like gunpowder, and came down the glen in the dark, singing song for song.' Campbell is found high in the top right-hand corner of the picture, looking like a younger Solzhenitsyn, with great domed head and long Russian-looking black beard – rather different from his calotype image where he stands, beardless, gazing reflectively into the distance with an outsize tall hat in his hand.

Women take a secondary role in the picture, as they did in the Disruption (and in life, except in the risky business of childbirth). High in the central part of the picture is Grace, the wife of Thomas Chalmers, with four of her six daughters beside her. Her eldest daughter, Anne, however, is found at the edge of the picture. Anne married William Hanna, the biographer of her father, also a minister, but in spite of these examples never felt at home in their Free Kirk. On the contrary, she was attracted by Catholicism, which must have alarmed them. When abroad, she liked to visit Catholic churches, dabbing her finger in the holy water as she entered, and crossing herself.

Anne was a slugabed. She loved to lie late in the morning, and seldom rose for breakfast but propped herself on the pillows reading, writing letters or receiving visitors, both male and female. She wrote lively letters and journals, and a brief memoir. Hill probably borrowed her likeness from the photograph which he and Adamson took of her reclining on a rustic seat in a garden.

Just above her is the elderly, hard-of-hearing Miss Charlotte Mackenzie of Seaforth, ear trumpet at the ready. She wears on her shawl one of 200 or so silver brooches distributed to commemorate the Disruption. The burning-bush emblem of the Church is the centrepiece, surrounded by thistles and significant dates in the Presbyterian calendar. A poem in the *Witness* gave it a plug: 'Wear the jewel, lady! Wear it on thy breast …'.

Looming large in the front row is the burly figure of Alexander Black, professor of theology at Marischal College in Aberdeen, with atlas open at the map of Palestine – which he visited on the Kirk's mission to the Holy Land. Beside him, John Duncan, known as Rabbi Duncan because of his work as a missionary among the Jews of Budapest. The son of a shoemaker, he fled the cobbler's last and found God as he crossed the bridge at Aberdeen: 'I stood in the street in an ecstasy of joy'. Now old, hunched, with a long white beard, he looks like a character in a fairytale – or maybe a Hebrew patriarch from the ghetto. He was notoriously scatterbrained, but so learned in languages that 'he could talk his way to the wall of China'. His faith was uncomplicated: he said that 'the best preaching is believe on Jesus Christ and keep the ten commandments'.

Rabbi Duncan puts a fatherly hand on a dark-haired boy beside him – Adolph Saphir, his first Jewish convert in Budapest. Adolph grew up to preach a Presbyterian gospel in Greenwich. Close by is Andrew Bonar, Black's fellow traveller to Palestine. The open book on his lap is his tribute to their late saintly companion, *Memoirs and Remains of R. M. McCheyne*. It was a bestseller. The man in the golden turban is Dhanjiobai Naurojie, a Parsee, one of the first converts from the Free Kirk mission to Bombay – Mumbai as it now is – who became a missionary in India.

Sir David Brewster, mentor of the St Andrews photographers, has a place near Chalmers and Welsh. He ignores them, and adjusts his specs as he reads his book. Brewster was in his sixties at the time of the Disruption and was already an embittered man. But life blossomed thirteen years later when, a few weeks short of his seventy-fifth birthday, travelling to the south of France, he met a young woman on her way with friends to winter in Nice. The elderly Brewster was smitten; he followed her, swept her off her feet, married, and set off with his Jane on an extended honeymoon in Italy. Good fortune followed him. He was appointed principal of Edinburgh University at the age of seventy-eight. (In that post he was called on to install as chancellor his old friend – and arch enemy of the Free Kirk – Henry, Lord Brougham, the man who had brought Hugh Miller's wrath on his head.)

There's James Young Simpson – Sir James by the time the picture was finished. A baker's son, professor of midwifery at Edinburgh, advocate of chloroform as an anaesthetic (despite opposition from bigots – suffering being the lot of man, and woman too). He was an elder in Thomas Guthrie's Free Church of St John (now St Columba's), along with Hugh Miller. It was Simpson's colleague, the surgeon John Miller – also in the picture – who performed the first operation with chloroform, cutting a tumour from the arm of a five-year-old boy from South Uist.

Nathaniel Paterson sits by a pillar. His claim to fame is ancestral, being a direct descendant of Old Mortality whose life's mission was to clean up the headstones of the Covenanting martyrs. Two of his nieces married well, one to

Jerome, Napoleon's youngest brother, the other to a nephew of the Duke of Wellington – a matrimonial entente cordiale of sorts. Paterson wrote a book called *The Manse Garden*, of which I know nothing. His neighbour is Richard Buchanan, whose hand rests on a three-volume *History of the Ten Years' Conflict*, Buchanan's own account of events leading up to the Disruption. It ran to many thousands of words, but neither Hugh Miller nor the *Witness* rated a single mention in it. Envy may be blamed for the omission. Buchanan edited an Evangelical newspaper overshadowed by Miller's.

In splendid profile, there is Alexander Dunlop, lawyer and later MP, bald on top but with curly ginger locks lapping his collar. The large document he holds is the Claim of Right which he drew up as the Evangelical answer to hostile verdicts in the courts. Dapper James Moncreiff strikes a pose with cane and top hat. Later, he'll be Lord Advocate. At the Disruption Assembly, he was a cross-bencher (i.e. one of the Forty Thieves) who sat tight while Chalmers led the walkout; but later, on second thoughts, he followed. The gentleman in the front row, whiskered and moustachioed, elegant in grey top coat and check trousers, with topper in one hand and a scroll in the other, is the Marquis of Breadalbane. He was Queen Victoria's chamberlain. Close by, with florid face and flowing locks, sits Fox Maule, MP (named after Charles James Fox, the great Whig politician). Fox Maule was a junior minister at Westminster before the Disruption, and secretary for war after it.

Sergeant Mackenzie, resplendent in kilt and scarlet tunic, pipe major of the 42nd Highlanders at Waterloo, is in place here as an officer of the Assembly. He is outranked by a number of other military men. There's Sir Thomas Makdougall Brisbane, a notable star-gazer. He soldiered in the Peninsula and reached the rank of major-general, after which he served as governor general in New South Wales – though he 'lacked energy'. He gave his name to Brisbane in Queensland. A passionate astronomer and builder of observatories (one at Sydney), he catalogued 7,000 stars. Two generals, a colonel and a captain (with a medal) are also visible.

Thomas Hately, the precentor, sits in the very foreground, hand on lips, with the psalter open on his lap and a tuning fork in his hat on the floor. Psalm-singing in the Free Kirk was unaccompanied (no organs, no 'kist of whistles' allowed), and the congregation followed the precentor's lead. Hately wrote several psalm tunes (his *Leuchars* is numbered 179 in the modern psalter).

Maitland Makgill Crichton of Rankeillor, 'the poor man's friend', landowner, lean and athletic, looks out from under his brows – he was a great pedestrian. He strode out from Elie in Fife alongside the mail coach and got to North Queensferry ahead of it.

Dr John Bruce, head atilt, was said to be the last man to preach in broad Scots. He was minister at St Andrew's church, where the 1843 Assembly met – an elegant place, where you might think to hear sermons in gentrified English. Look on his face in the picture, and then at the minister in Harvey's painting *Quitting the Manse* – the same! Hill copied it, probably from the photograph; and so, it seems, did Harvey.

Sir George Harvey was president of the Royal Scottish Academy by the time the picture was painted, and cured at last from the effects of a troublesome accident. He toppled from a gig, hit his head on the causeway, and for ten years thereafter suffered from headaches, impaired vision and bouts of depression; he tried homoeopathy, hydropathy and a holiday in the Italian sunshine, all in vain, but was restored to vigour when Hill's brother-in-law Joseph Noel Paton found him a good doctor.

Look closely on another face, just squeezed in at the bottom right-hand corner. Is it … can it be Robert Burns? No, look again. It's *Thomas* Burns, nephew of the poet. The likeness is close, but not the sentiments. Nephew Burns, a minister of the Kirk, came out at the Disruption and preached to his people in a farmyard at Monkton in Ayrshire. Soon after that, he set sail for New Zealand to minister to the Scots emigrants of Otago, all Free Kirkers (and made his landfall at Port Chalmers, named after the great man).

Dr James Begg, father of social housing in Edinburgh ('Happy Homes for Working Men'), is there. In the Colonies, as they're known, there are streets named after Free Kirk heroes – Hugh Miller Place in Stockbridge, for example. Also John Syme, minister of Free Greyfriars, whose life was changed by a talk in Calton Jail with an immigrant Highlander about to be hanged for murder. Syme was so horrified by his tale of destitution and the debauchery in the evil dens of the city that he started a campaign for decent lodging houses that spread to other towns and other lands.

Robert Walter Stewart, the man who dashed from Constantinople to get to the Disruption in time, finds a spot in the top right-hand corner. He sports a forked beard. Since his health was poor, he spent the latter part of his life in Italy, ministering in Leghorn to the large body of Italian Protestants and the shifting population of the busy port.

Patrick Clason's snowy beard, flecked with auburn, rolls in splendid waves to his chest. He was a high-minded man – he considered earthly pursuits vain; all will perish. Robert Gordon, once of St Giles, looks saintlike with his downcast eyes and folded hands. He was said to resemble pictures of Shakespeare (he doesn't). Mrs Menteith had a literary talent, being the 'charming authoress' of poems on the early Scottish church. Horatio Bonnar wrote *Hymns of Faith and Hope*: 'I heard the voice of Jesus say', 'Glory be to God the father', and many more. Or, as Hill wrote in his key to the picture in 1866 when he could no longer put a name to all of the faces: 'etc., etc., etc.'.

There are notable absentees. Among the missing is John Swanson, itinerant minister of the Small Isles, cabined with Hugh Miller for six weeks on board the *Betsey*. And why not Miller's wife, Lydia? So many other wives are there, most of them present, I suspect, by reason of their husbands. Lydia Miller – 'My Lydia' – was an author in her own right. She wrote one of the few novels to feature the Disruption, *Passages in the Life of an English heiress, or Recollections of Disruption Times in Scotland*, published anonymously in 1847 and now sunk without trace. Novel-writing and reading were ill-thought-of by strict Presbyterians, fiction being considered tantamount to lying. Lydia, as 'Mrs Myrtle', wrote stories for children. Also absent is George Buchan of Kelloe. Buchan made regular appearances at the Kirk's Assemblies as an elder but missed the Disruption, having been thrown from his horse at his home in the Borders. Earlier in life, he'd been saved from a shipwreck – maybe he was accident-prone. Buchan was a benevolent laird, giving coal, food, clothes, cordials and money to the poor – at least, to the 'deserving' poor. (Thomas Chalmers would have recognised the distinction.) He had a proper sense of priorities. At one Assembly, when a vote of thanks to Chalmers was proposed for his eloquence, Buchan moved that first they should give thanks to God.

It may be that only 100 or so of these likenesses directly replicated calotype images, though the number may be higher. Hill may have sketched from the life in some cases, or used other portraits as a guide where no Hill and Adamson photographs had been taken.

On completion of his picture, Hill outlined a key to it, numbering and identifying most but not all of the faces. The gaps suggest that, in the long interval between conception and completion, Hill lost some of his notes. Who is the woman perched in the topmost right-hand corner? Or the two below her, one half-hidden in deep shade? Sisters forever nameless.

There's a man in a wideawake hat silhouetted against the light of an open door at the top edge of the painting – and him we know, though he's neither named nor numbered in the key. He's Thomas Annan, a Glasgow photographer, celebrated heir to the Hill and Adamson partnership and a close friend of Hill. He looks as if he's squeezed in at the last minute, which is what happened, at least in paint. Hill added him to the picture as a thank-you.

17

Who'll buy?

It was a little late. Twenty-three years had passed since engravings from 'a picture to be painted by D. O. Hill, Esq., RSA' had been advertised for sale. They were to have been available in two to three years' time. Now that the picture was painted, Hill still hoped to sell copies to the public. But engraving was a slow and expensive process and there was new technology to hand which made the engraver redundant. Photography had come of age.

So Hill was now able to announce that arrangements had been made with 'that admirable photographer Mr Thomas Annan' for reproducing the picture in several sizes, using the new method of carbon photography which 'secures the impression from evanescence and renders it permanent' – in other words, photos guaranteed not to fade. Readers of Hill's prospectus *The Disruption of the Church of Scotland: An Historical Picture* 'containing four hundred and fifty portraits' were told that Annan had already produced a large number of negatives of 'consummate excellence', using the new large camera he had ordered from an eminent optician.

Hill's art-dealer brother Alexander was no longer at hand to sell the prints, as was first intended. He had died that June. But another agency had been found, and purchasers were invited to place their orders at an 'office of the Disruption picture' at 16 Royal Exchange. The venture was successful, and soon a large framed photograph of D. O. Hill's great painting could be found in many a Free Kirk home. As noted previously, Thomas Annan himself appears among the Disruption worthies, having – as it were – sneaked into his own photograph by the grace of Mr Hill.

The question was, who would buy the painting? The *Scotsman*, which two years earlier had advocated its acquisition by the Scottish National Gallery so that the nation should own and the people see such an important historical work, now took a different line: 'Doubtless, the Free Kirk, which is wise in its generation, will take good care to possess itself of this record of its birth'.

And so it happened, though not without a quibble over the asking price. Hill had taken the precaution of seeking the advice of his friend Sir George Harvey, president of the Royal Academy. Harvey fixed on 3,000 guineas as a suitable fee, and robustly defended it when questioned. He calculated that painting the picture had taken Hill the equivalent of ten years' uninterrupted work, and therefore the estimate was modest – 'surely a moderate return for the exercise of the talents of so gifted a person as Mr Hill during the very best period of his life'.

Free Kirk leaders leapt to Hill's defence at that year's Assembly. Robert Candlish expressed the fear that if they didn't buy the painting it might be snapped up by some other party, probably American, and would disappear across the Atlantic. And this was true: Lyman Beecher, father of Harriet Beecher Stowe, who had attended the 1843 Assembly and had also seen the finished picture, was prepared to raise funds in the States if the Kirk didn't buy. Robert Buchanan pointed to the regrettable absence of any memorial of the first Assembly of the Kirk after its foundation by John Knox, 'with all the remarkable men who sat with him'; this time they should not let the opportunity slip. Dr James Begg demanded that it should be bought at once and toured through all the towns of Scotland. A bargain was struck for the lesser sum of £1,500, made up mainly from subscriptions of £100 from well-heeled wellwishers.

Dr Begg carried the day. Once acquired, the picture was taken on a progress round the country – Glasgow and Greenock were among the stopping places – before being drawn up the Mound to its resting place in Presbytery Hall in the Free Kirk college. There were two more public appearances. In 1888 it was taken to Inverness, where the Assembly was held that year, to be the star exhibit at a show of Disruption relics. Because of its size, special arrangements had to be made by the railway officials.

Since then, too heavy and bulky to be easily moved, it has remained a fixture in Edinburgh, apart from a trip to London when it was shown at the Royal Academy in 1970. Hopes of making it the centrepiece of an exhibition at the Scottish National Portrait Gallery in 2002, the bicentenary of Hill's birth, came to nought because of the expense – a pity, since it would have given the public a rare chance of seeing it to advantage, with easy access. It remains a picture more talked about than seen.

Confronted with the picture at the private viewing, Sir George Harvey was measured in his praise. It was a noble work, a precious bequest to future generations of the Free Church. It was 'unique of its kind; I know of nothing like it existing'. But how good was it as a work of art? He didn't say.

Harvey set the pattern. Since then, there has been little but faint praise at the best, and sometimes scorn for Hill's great gamble with destiny. Charles Heath Wilson saw Hill at work on the painting in the early years and was at least hopeful: 'I thought you a little crazy when I heard of it, but you have proved what heart of sentiment can do'. Writing from London, where he was director of the art schools at Somerset House, he told Hill: 'I often think about it and hope earnestly that you may succeed'. This was a wary testimonial.

Once lodged in the Free Church Hall, in a sort of limbo where it was visible only on request and seen only by a few of the faithful and the occasional art historian, the picture ceased to attract attention. Later comments were no more than lukewarm. Robert Brydall in his influential *Art in Scotland* (1889) declared that 'such a work afforded no scope for artistic treatment'. John Stuart Blackie, professor of Greek at Edinburgh University, who described Hill as his 'great friend among artists' (next to Harvey), reflected in later years: 'He made a great mistake in middle life by undertaking an historical picture of the Free Church Disruption, which he removed altogether out of the province of art by making it a gallery of portraits instead of a single effective group'. This, succinctly, is the view of all Hill's critics. Blackie went on to regret that 'the labour he devoted to this work took away several of the best years of his life, and when it was finished it remained a mere historical curiosity, for which he received neither fame as an artist nor money as a merchant'. An early critic referred to it as the 'weary' Disruption picture, 'which must have lain like an incubus on his genius'.

The most scathing comment of all came from Sam Bough, Hill's younger contemporary and fellow academician, who had a rough jocular tongue. Bough put it about that he'd written satirical verses on the picture which he threatened to print (he didn't – if they existed). He was reported to have criticised the painting's flaws in 'a very comical manner', dismissing Hill's rank upon rank of animated faces as 'potatoes all in a row'. But Bough was no friend of Hill.

More recent commentators have been kinder, though seldom favourable in their judgements. For instance, the German critic Heinrich Schwarz: 'He squandered his marvellous and inspired portrait photographs on a frigid setting and a huge and clumsy background'. Others have called the work 'a misspent labour of love' and 'the most impressive bad painting produced in nineteenth-century Scotland'.

For the art historian and critic Duncan Macmillan, the Disruption picture turned out to be 'a cumbersome group portrait'. And Sara Stevenson, whose critical biography and many studies of Hill (with or without Adamson) provide the most comprehensive assessment of his life and work, responds regretfully that 'we feel the failure of the painting, partly because the photographs are so much better'. As curator of the photography collection at the Scottish National Portrait Gallery, it is the last consideration which interests her most.

> It is probable that his enthusiasm for photography, rather than acting as an aid, effectively ruined his great Free Church painting. His original sketches for the painting are far livelier and involved a smaller, more manageable group of people; the final result took more than twenty years' labour, and included more than four hundred recognisable portraits painted accurately and laboriously from the calotypes. The result is historically interesting rather than impressive, and lacks the emotional force of the calotypes themselves.

This is true, and it couldn't be otherwise. Even when the Hill and Adamson group portraits were taken without thought for aesthetic effect, but only to provide models for the painting, they have a freshness and vitality that belies the deadening effect of a long exposure time. You feel that the half-dozen or so people involved have a reason to be together, share a common interest, are engaged in some purpose of the moment. Take, for example, one very early calotype of ministers surrounding Thomas Chalmers, seated and standing: the pose is static, the last of the twenty-four figures fade to nothingness, and the photograph is technically flawed – yet there's more life in it than Hill could hope to achieve in his unmanageable painting.

Hill built a vivid sense of drama into some of his group photographs, to a script of his own devising. Professor Alexander Campbell Fraser expounds, hand outstretched, apparently to a tutorial of attentive young ministers. A group of eight men (names mostly unknown) are clearly at cross purposes – but why? – four of them in animated conversation, one grandly indifferent. Hugh Miller sits reading, head bowed, while Hill crouches beside him and three others look on – one with a plaid round his shoulder, another standing, coolly observant with hand on hip, in tartan waistcoat and loud check trews. (Stylish dress always helped. Black-backed ministers were more of a problem.)

Once Hill had seen the potential of calotype photography, even those relatively simple photographs taken for use as working sketches for the painting can be seen as works of art in their own right. When he and Adamson aimed at artistic effect, the results were often astounding. To take three examples: a street scene with fisherwomen in St Andrews; a luminous group portrait of Thomas Chalmers and his family in the garden at Merchiston Castle; and a strange, unearthly composition of Highland soldiers arranged round a bronze cannon in a battery at Edinburgh Castle. These are Hill's true masterpieces.

In an article in the *Witness* headed 'The Calotype', in July 1843, Hugh Miller first made the comparison with Raeburn, the great Scottish portraitist of the previous generation, which later writers were to echo. Having seen the first results of Hill and Adamson's photographic work, he enthused over the haunting new images they produced and the almost impressionistic effect dictated by the calotype medium. One likeness of Thomas Chalmers (his hero) he characterised as 'exactly after the manner of Raeburn. There is the same broad freedom of touch; no nice miniature stipplings, as if laid in by the point of a needle – no sharp-edged strokes; all is solid, massy, broad.'

He compared that photograph to an engraved portrait of Chalmers, and found the latter wanting. 'We have placed a head of Dr Chalmers taken in this way [i.e., the calotype]', he wrote, 'beside one of the most powerful prints of him yet given to the public, and find from the contrast that the latter, with all its power, is but a mere approximation.' It was the calotype that spoke true. Another photograph was described by Miller as 'exactly after the manner of Raeburn'.

The Hill and Adamson portraits sometimes brought another old master to mind. When the landscape and marine artist Clarkson Stanfield was given a collection of the calotypes, he commented that he 'would rather have a set of them than the finest Rembrandts [he meant engravings] I ever saw'. And Hill himself referred to one of the calotype portraits as 'singularly Rembrandtish'. The Raeburn/Rembrandt comparison still holds good. Duncan Macmillan in his book *Scottish Art 1460–2000* writes that the calotypes, though thoroughly modern, 'clearly look back to Raeburn and beyond him to Rembrandt'.

This could be attributed partly to the calotype medium. 'Broadly speaking, Raeburn's practice was to dramatise contrasts of dark and light', writes a present-day critic. 'By coincidence, the calotype process produces Raeburnesque effects.'

Sir David Brewster, originally the enthusiastic sponsor of the Adamson brothers in their work on the calotype, soon transferred his allegiance to the daguerreotype precisely because of the 'flaws' inherent in the calotype process and the uncertainty of the technique. He was particularly sharp in his condemnation of the calotype as a method of portraiture. Likenesses were too often 'hideous', no less, 'even when female beauty has submitted to its martyrdom'. He elaborated: 'This defect arises, to a certain extent, from the rough grain, so to speak, of the paper, and also to its imperfect transparency – for in the positive every imperfection of the paper is copied, and every luminous point re-appears as a black one – so that the positive picture has the appearance of being stippled, as it were, with grains of sand, which give a painful appearance to the human face'.

It was true. If the ideal was a Raphael madonna or Alan Ramsay's Margaret Lindsay, then what Miller called 'this little brown drawing' fell far short of perfection, and Hill had martyred his unfortunate female sitters. In the light of much modern portraiture with its deliberate distortions, or considering that many contemporary photographers aim at a grainy quality of print, the criticism loses much of its sting. George Harvey rose to Hill's defence. Referring to the stippling effect which Brewster had objected to so vehemently, he pointed out that similar roughness could be seen in fine chalk drawings.

Hill was well aware of the chance element in the calotypes – 'the possibilities of accident and the subtle and interesting warp of a process slightly out of control', as Sara Stevenson has it. When the so-called deficiencies of calotype compared to the daguerreotype process were used to belittle his efforts, Hill responded defiantly. The daguerreotype, though it seemed to be an exact reproduction of nature, was at best 'the much diminished work of God', while the broad-stroke pictures which he and Adamson produced were 'the imperfect work of a man' – and that, he claimed proudly, 'was the very life of it'.

'There is no poetry in the pencil of the sun', said Brewster, using a familiar contemporary metaphor. Hill disagreed. He used the sun to maximum effect in the photograph of Chalmers and his family in the grounds of Merchiston Castle. Only Chalmers faces the camera directly, the bright sunlight which rakes across the group casting one side of his regal head into deep shadow and backlighting his crown of white hair. This picture, according to Sara Stevenson, takes Hill into regions beyond Raeburn. 'Knowing the difficulties involved, Hill, far from adapting to them, has exaggerated the problem by pushing the coarse character of the process close to abstraction'. She finds another example in the calotype which Hill and Adamson took of Highland soldiers at Edinburgh Castle. A drum in the foreground is the most sharply focused detail in a photograph in which much is soft and fuzzy. Above it gapes a cannon mouth.

The drummer leans on the gun barrel, drumsticks in hand. The eye comes naturally to rest on a soldier's craggy, rough-hewn features – the only face clearly seen amid an abstract pattern of dark feather bonnets and dazzling white cross-belts.

We can't know what Hill felt about his Disruption painting. He never spoke frankly about it.

No regrets? He began with almost youthful zest, but some-where along the road his inspiration faltered or his nerve failed. Meanwhile, as he struggled to make progress on the big picture, and was otherwise occupied with the business of the Academy, his career as a landscape painter stalled.

It's clear that he should have stuck with his early ideas, as revealed in the tantalising preliminary sketches. He needed a hero, and that hero could only have been Thomas Chalmers. Instead, he was trapped by the urge to add more and yet more identifiable faces to his ever-extending canvas – a commitment made relatively early, as Hugh Miller revealed in an article written three years after Hill began the work. Miller remarked on 'the doubling of the scale of the picture, and the insertion of twice or three times the number of portraits than were at first contemplated'. As a result, Hill ended up with a disastrous crush of figures at the extremities – a visual log-jam – and an absence of drama at the centre.

Two paintings by Sir David Wilkie probably influenced Hill's first notions of what the picture should be. Most clearly, there is Wilkie's *John Knox Preaching at St Andrews*, in which Knox, from his position high and off-centre in the canvas, energetically thrusts out an arm in a moment of passion, to an audience disposed in knots and groups around him. There's plenty of evidence that Chalmers, as both preacher in the pulpit and orator on the platform, threw himself into the part, with lively expression and dramatic gestures. Hill seemed to be aiming at that in one or two of his sketches. But, in the picture, Chalmers stands subdued, reflective and withdrawn, no fire burning. This is much as he appears in the calotype photographs, the result, no doubt, of having to hold a pose as the seconds and minutes of the long exposure time ticked by.

Hill studied Wilkie's unfinished *John Knox Administering the Sacrament at Calder House* closely. Here Knox stands at the centre of a long table, goblet in hand, among a rich diversity of characters. Hill's early pen-and-wash drawing of the Disruption scene bears a tenuous resemblance to it. But alas, he crowded out the initial idea.

When less than half-way into the painting of his picture, Hill was touched by self-doubt on seeing a vast canvas by the French romantic painter Paul Delaroche exhibited in Edinburgh. 'I wish I had seen the original ten years ago', he said; 'my Free Kirk picture would in that case long ago have been done.' He must have been referring to the head count rather than the subject matter, for Delaroche's seventy or so characters in motley include some bare-chested males and a couple of bare-breasted females. Hill's Presbyterian ladies are decently covered to the chin and none bare-headed (all those women in their bonnets resemble, in another context, headscarved Muslims).

If only Hill had chosen another, more dramatic, moment from the Disruption proceedings. He might have shown Chalmers addressing the Assembly, or the exodus from St Andrew's church into thronged George Street, or the arrival of the godly multitude at Tanfield with the river running by. Hill's contemporary, the artist William Bonnar, depicted both the latter scenes, but without Hill's flair.

Hill was sadly hampered by the static nature of his subject, which is the problem facing all illustrators of great formal occasions. Not for him the animation of Wilkie's *Chelsea Pensioners Reading the Waterloo Despatch* – 'history in terms of the experience of ordinary people', as Duncan Macmillan has written. Figures cluster round a table in front of a roadside inn while one of their number reads out the despatch. Excitement, anticipation and glee are reflected in their faces. Dogs yap, a trooper on horseback – the bearer of the tidings – twists athletically in the saddle, an ardent young officer hoists up his infant, onlookers thrust their heads from a window, girls wave their kerchiefs.

None of these characters were 'original portraits'. When Wilkie did have to assemble known people in his *The First Council of Queen Victoria*, the notables who attended the girl queen included two royal dukes, two archbishops, Lord Melbourne (the prime minister), Wellington and Peel – but there were only thirty of them, not 400. Charles Greville makes a telling point about this picture. 'The likenesses are generally pretty good, but it is a very unfaithful representation of what actually took place', he wrote in his journal, noting that there were actually ninety-seven privy councillors present. 'He has introduced as many figures as he well could, but has made a strong selection.' As it turned out, selection was not Hill's forte.

When Jacques-Louis David, painter to the French revolutionaries, made his vast sketch for *The Tennis Club Oath* (the painting was never finished), he filled the crowded picture with anonymous faces apart from the figures in the foreground. Mirabeau leaps to his feet in an ecstasy of patriotism. Melodramatic poses are struck, arms flung upwards, hats tossed in the air, citizens embrace. It's history as histrionics.

Macmillan suggests that Hill may have known David's work and borrowed from it; his spectators in the skylights at Tanfield may have been suggested by the raggle-taggle onlookers clustered at the windows of the (real, not lawn) tennis court. There may be another, subconscious, link. David's National Assembly members, having been locked out of their ornate chamber, marched defiantly through the rain to meet in a bare sports hall; seceding Scottish Evangelicals quit the Assembly in handsome St Andrew's for a utilitarian shed at Tanfield.

In the end, it's not the lack of action that damns the Disruption picture. It's the lack of organisation. There's a work by Goya called *Junta of the Philippines*, painted about 1815, which is even larger than Hill's picture and equally static. Thirteen people sit in line at a table on a dais (one lit by a beam of sunlight), flanked by two groups seated along the side walls. That's all – except that the figures are dwarfed by the towering walls. Goya's latest biographer Robert Hughes draws attention to the 'deliberate cultivation of mystery in the middle of what, by rights, should have been a straightforward narrative of an official event'.

There is nothing of that sort in the Disruption picture. But there's mystery in a little framed sketch in oils that Hill painted beforehand. The colour is dark except where a few highlights are dotted in white. The paint has been hastily and thickly daubed, and any detail is blurred. It's just possible to make out a shadowy gesturing figure (who must be Thomas Chalmers) and another at the table below. A shaft of golden light pierces the gloom.

This is the germ of the big picture. But in the sketch the hall itself is the dominant feature. The walls and ceiling – bare as a prison – enclose and arch over the tiny humans. It's a powerful symbol, and suitably Presbyterian: these are mere mortals in the presence of an awesome God.

18

The artist in his element

The Free Kirk is not what it was when Hill first put pencil to pad at Tanfield. Patronage, the rock on which the Church split, ceased to be an issue by the latter part of the nineteenth century. The Moderate party in the Church of Scotland withered. But the Free Church, glorying in its independence and settled in its kirks and manses, proud of its schools and missions and comfortable in all its guid gear, was in no mood to compromise. In 1900, the bulk of its members felt sufficiently amenable to merge with another protesting branch of the Presbyterian faith (there have been many – the history of Scotch Presbyterianism is a tangle of fissions and fusions) under the name United Free Church; and at last, in the third decade of the twentieth century, that body linked hands with the auld enemy in a reborn Church of Scotland.

Which way would Thomas Chalmers have turned? Who knows – it's an idle speculation. But a remnant of diehards held out from both these amalgamations and still bears the name Free Church of Scotland, first coined in the heroic days of 1843. They claim to be the true heirs of that great popular movement. Now sadly diminished in numbers and influence, this rump of a great tradition is mainly confined to the Highlands and islands, and is often referred to by outsiders – in terms that may be scathing or affectionate according to choice – as the Wee Frees. But in one sense the Wee Frees are sitting pretty. After a long legal tussle, they gained ownership of the valuable Free Kirk college at the top of the Mound, and within it the picture.

'This famous painting is internationally important as being the first work of art painted with the help of a camera' – so says the caption on a reproduction of Hill's picture sold in the Free Kirk bookshop. Later artists eagerly made use of the camera to help realise their vision, though not everyone owned up to it; and, in the words of a recent writer, 'only rarely did an artist like Degas admit to what was in fact a widespread practice'.

One of the earliest to use a photograph as a prop was the Scottish portraitist Charles Lees, an exact contemporary of Hill (he was elected to the Scottish Academy in the same year as D. O.). He borrowed a calotype image of golfers at St Andrews, taken by Hill and Adamson probably in 1845, for the central group in his painting *The Golfers: A Grand Match Played over the Links of St Andrews on the Day of the Annual Meeting of the Royal and Ancient Golf Club* (recently acquired by the Scottish National Portrait Gallery). The focus of the painting is an animated circle of spectators watching the progress of a top-hatted gentleman's putt as the ball rolls towards the hole (he sank it, we learn elsewhere). The scene is almost a mirror image of the photograph, particularly the half-crouching figure of the rubicund putter, Hugh Lyon Playfair, a future captain of the Royal & Ancient, provost of St Andrews, and enthusiastic dabbler in calotype photography in the company of Sir David Brewster and the Adamson brothers.

At least three other Scottish artists either copied directly from Hill and Adamson calotype images or used them as a guide. Sir George Harvey made use of photographs taken at Greyfriars' church in Edinburgh. David Roberts, friend and correspondent of Hill, 'borrowed' a group of Hill and Adamson soldiers. John Watson Gordon painted a posthumous portrait of

Sir William Allan based on his calotype image. Likewise, when John Maclaren Barclay painted the Rev. Andrew Gray preaching (the picture is in Perth Art Gallery), he replicated a Hill and Adamson photograph. He couldn't paint Gray from life, since the man had been thirteen years in his grave by then.

It seems likely that John (later Sir John) Lavery used photographs to great effect in his vast picture showing Queen Victoria among a host of glittering guests at the Glasgow exhibition of 1888. Lavery had been commissioned to record the scene and to include likenesses of more than 250 people present in the pavilion at Kelvingrove Park. Lavery was there, seated in a curtained-off vantage point, where he dashed off a rough sketch of the scene which is now in Aberdeen Art Gallery. Evidence has come to light that he and his friend James Craig Annan, son of Thomas Annan, may have hatched a scheme to facilitate the task. Annan arranged portrait sessions with the guests, allowing Lavery use of the prints to supplement his own sketches. Lavery never spoke of this, no doubt fearful for his reputation as a creative artist if the news got out; but in this way he was able to complete his portrait studies within two years. (This is the startling suggestion of Brian Thom McQuade, who recently unearthed a heap of Annan's plate-glass negatives in a dusty box in the cellar of Glasgow Art Club, and made the connection.)

David Octavius Hill died in May 1870, just before Assembly time. Ill-health had forced him to give up the secretaryship of the Academy the year before. There were the customary tributes to his life and work. The engineer James Nasmyth, referring some time later to his dear and 'most agreeable friend and companion' David *Oswald* Hill (a lapse), remembered him as the incarnation of geniality, recalling his lively sense of humour and his 'romantic and poetic constitution of mind'. In his memoirs, his praise of Hill as an artist was modified; though he had been a fine draughtsman, 'somehow, when he came to handle the brush, the result was not always satisfactory – a defect not uncommon with artists'. The point can be argued. 'Contrary to received opinion, the picture is in fact well painted' (Duncan Macmillan).

The Academy in its annual report for 1870 mourned the loss of an 'excellent secretary' and regretted that he had not been spared to further the prosperity of the institution he loved. But not a word about his artistic merit. 'Poor Hill', exclaims the academy's historian Esmé Gordon – though he'd shown more than 270 paintings at academy exhibitions, though he'd received so many commissions, though the queen had bought one of his works – 'of his art, his prints, photographic and lithographic, of his achievements – nothing.'

'Mr Hill fought the battles of the Academy with a singleness of purpose and a devotion of time and talent', wrote an obituarist, adding that in effect this had 'impaired his efforts towards attaining that first-rate place in art otherwise in reach of his fertile and felicitous genius'.

Hill's widow Amelia sculpted his likeness on the gravestone at Dean cemetery, and her bust of him is in the Scottish National Gallery. But it's in the numerous photographs taken during his lifetime, and particularly the calotypes, that Hill is best seen – either on his own or with others in a group. They are the best monument to the man, better than bronze or marble.

One other likeness.

Come. Walk up the Mound. See the brass plate: 'Free Church college and offices'. Enter the cramped lobby. Press a button to call the caretaker from his cubicle. Climb two flights of stairs, or take the antique lift. If walking, notice the portraits and pictures on the walls: the severe dame in black; the solemn gent, ditto; a composite photo of the bearded few who held to their heritage in 1900. Also an ascending line of small landscape prints, engraved from scenes by D. O. Hill.

A door in the bare corridor opens on to a scene of un-expected richness: this is Presbytery Hall, jewel in a plain setting, a large room glowing with the warm lustre of panelled walls – Oregon pine, brought from the American west in one of the earliest shipments. Pairs of fluted pilasters in the same wood line the walls. The coffered ceiling is picked out with gold leaf, and light floods from a great coloured glass window.

This is where the Disruption picture hangs. Search among the faces, find the painter: David Octavius Hill in his golden-haired prime, above his partner Robert Adamson, with his friends around him, in the company of the elect.

Notes and sources

Sara Stevenson's *The Personal Art of David Octavius Hill* (Yale University Press, 2002) covers the whole field and is the essential source for any study of the artist; it has been my constant source of reference. I refer to it in these notes as 'Stevenson, *Personal Art*'. Quotation from Hill's correspondence in his 'well-known *illegible* hand' has been made possible thanks to Sara Stevenson's labours in the archives, including that of the National Library of Scotland, and subsequent citation in her several works. Robin H. Rodger's succinct *The Remarkable Mr Hill* (Perth Museum and Art Gallery, 2002) is also informative ('Rodger, *Mr Hill*'). In the matter of early photography, Sara Stevenson's *David Octavius Hill and Robert Adamson: A Catalogue of their Calotypes in the Collection of the Scottish National Portrait Gallery* (Scottish National Portrait Gallery, 1981) is indispensable ('Stevenson, *Catalogue*') – see also work by Larry J. Schaaf cited below.

I have benefited from Duncan Macmillan's discussion of Hill's Disruption painting, and from illuminating comments on fellow artists and their work, in his *Scottish Art 1460–2000* (Mainstream, 2000) ('Macmillan, *Scottish Art*') and in his detailed study of 'The Disruption Painting' referred to below.

Essays collected in *Scotland in the Age of the Disruption* (Edinburgh University Press, 1993), particularly those by the editors Stewart J. Brown and Michael Fry, set social, religious and political affairs in context, and two further collections address more specific themes: *The Practical and the Pious: Essays on Thomas Chalmers*, edited by A. C. Cheyne (Saint Andrew Press, 1985) ('Cheyne, *Essays*'), and *Hugh Miller and the Controversies of Victorian Science,* edited by Michael Shortland (Oxford University Press, 1996) ('Shortland, *Controversies*').

There is no full-scale modern biography of Thomas Chalmers, the leader of the Disruption. *Memoirs of Thomas Chalmers* (1854), by his son-in-law William Hanna ('Hanna, *Memoirs*'), is voluminous and reverential. Hugh Miller has fared better. George Rosie's *Hugh Miller: Outrage and Order* (Mainstream, 1981) ('Rosie, *Hugh Miller*') combines brief biography with passages from Miller's writings – an excellent introduction to the stonemason turned savant. *Celebrating the Life and Times of Hugh Miller*, a compilation of papers based on the bicentenary conference organised by the Cromarty Arts Trust and the Elphinstone Institute of the University of Aberdeen at Cromarty in October 2002, edited by Lester Borley, is copiously informative. I refer to it as 'Borley, *Celebrating*'. Robert Adamson's brief life, alas, can only be glimpsed from the few references made by his friends; some I quote.

Some other principal sources:

J. H. S. Burleigh, *A Church History of Scotland* (Oxford University Press, 1960), summarises the Disruption, its causes, course and consequences ('Burleigh, *Church History*'); Esmé Gordon, *The Royal Scottish Academy of Painting, Sculpture and Architecture* (Charles Skilton, 1976) ('Gordon, *RSA*'); A. D. Morrison-Low and J. R. R. Christie (eds), *Martyr of Science: Sir David Brewster 1781–1806* (Royal Scottish Museum, 1984) ('Morrison-Low and Christie, *Martyr*'); *Studies in Photography*, special number, edited by Ray McKenzie and Monica Thorp (Scottish Society for the History of Photography, 2003), being proceedings of the 2002 Edinburgh conference 'The Artful Use of Light' ('McKenzie and Thorp, *Studies*).

The *Witness*, the Free Church newspaper edited by Hugh Miller, is a mine of (sometimes partisan) information.

Abbreviations

NLS   National Library of Scotland

NMPFT   National Museum of Photography, Film
            and Television

RSA   Royal Scottish Academy

Chapter 1   Picture on the wall

Two pamphlets offer detailed descriptions of Hill's Disruption
picture and its subjects: *The Disruption of the Church of Scotland:
An Historical Picture* (1866), published anonymously but
presumed to be by Hill ('Hill, *Historical Picture*'), and *The
Disruption Picture: A Memorial of the First General Assembly of the
Free Church of Scotland* by Donald MacKinnon (Free Church of
Scotland, 1943) ('Mackinnon, *Disruption Picture*').

Chapter 2   Farewell to Egypt

Reports in the *Witness* newspaper describe the events of
Disruption day in detail. The *Scotsman* predicted that 'there will
be no disruption in the church' on 17 May 1843, and recalled
Bute's ill-informed reassurances to Peel, the prime minister (31
May 1843).

The Rev. Adam White's slow progress from the northern
isles can be inferred from a letter to the *Witness*, 20 May
1843; Robert Kernohan drew my attention to Robert Walter
Stewart's dash across Europe. Black dress for clergymen was
advertised for sale in the *Witness*, 20 May 1843.

Margaret Oliphant's description of crowds filling the
church is from her *Thomas Chalmers: Preacher, Philosopher and
Statesman* (1893) ('Oliphant, *Chalmers*'). References to the

life and character of the Rev. David Welsh, 'named after the sweet singer of Israel', are from James Aitken Wylie's *Disruption Worthies: A Memorial of 1843* (1876) ('Wylie, *Worthies*').

Chapter 3   O for Octavius

This chapter owes much to Sara Stevenson's study of David Octavius Hill's life and engaging personality ('unfailingly attractive') in her *Personal Art*, and has also benefited from Robert H. Rodger's *Mr Hill*. Hill's association with the Scottish (later Royal Scottish) Academy is detailed in Gordon, *RSA*. Hill's correspondence as secretary of the Academy is in the Royal Scottish Academy archive at the Dean Gallery, Edinburgh.

Hill described his 'splitting headache' in a letter to Joseph Noel Paton, 19 November 1851 (NLS, Acc. 11315). Henry Cockburn's description of himself as 'a frivolous dog' is from *Some Letters of Lord Cockburn*, edited by Henry A. Cockburn (1910), quoted in Stevenson, *Personal Art*. Hill's 'sweet and deep tones', both as painter and singer, were praised by John Brown in a review (of Ruskin) in *North British Review*, vol. 6 (1848), where he also referred to Hill's 'fine frenzy' while sketching. Hill was described as a 'seriously minded' churchman of 'profound convictions' in Mackinnon, *Disruption Picture* and Hill's sombre reflections on mortality are quoted from his correspondence with David Roberts and with John and Jane Macdonald (NLS, Acc. 11782 and 1742). The words of Hill's dizzy dancing partner are quoted in Stevenson, *Personal Art*, from a undated memoir by Margaret Saunders of Dundee in the collection of Dr Patrick Mullin.

Hill's 'careful observation of the play of light', remarked on by Amelia Hill and quoted in Stevenson, *Personal Art*, is from Mrs William Sharp, 'D. O. Hill, RSA', in *Camera Work*, no. 28 (October 1909). The friend who sympathised with Hill for his rheumatic right hand – and upbraided him for his handwriting – is John Macrone in a letter to Hill, 10 January 1848 (NLS, Acc. 11608). The profusion of engravings made from Hill's work was noted by Robert Brydall in his *Art in Scotland* (1889) ('Brydall, *Art in Scotland*').

Excerpts from Hill's official correspondence in connection with RSA exhibitions are quoted from MS copies of letters in the Letter Book 1826–1832, RSA archives – to Constable and Turner, both December 1831; and to Wilkie on the safe arrival of his painting, 8 February 1832, and its enthusiastic reception, 16 July 1832. References to the Dick Lauder debacle and McIan's complaint are from Gordon, *RSA*.

Chapter 4   Pleased to meet Mr Adamson

For Brewster and the St Andrews circle, see Morrison-Low and Christie, *Martyr*; also A. D. Morrison-Low, 'Brewster, Talbot and the Adamsons: the arrival of photography in St Andrews', in *History of Photography*, vol. 25, no. 2, summer (2001); and her 'Sir David Brewster and Photography' in *Review of Scottish Culture*, 4 (1988). See also Stevenson, *Personal Art*.

'I got hold of the artist ...': letter from David Brewster to Henry Fox Talbot, 3 July 1843, NMPFT 1937-4926, quoted in Sara Stevenson, *Facing the Light: The Photography of Hill and Adamson* (Scottish National Portrait Gallery, 2002). Henry Cockburn described Brewster's talent for making enemies in his *Circuit Journeys* (1884), quoted by A. D. Morrison-Low, 'Brewster and scientific instruments', in Morrison-Low and Christie, *Martyr*; Morrison-Low quotes the similar opinion expressed by 'another' (Elizabeth Grant of Rothiemurchus) from Jane M. Strachey, *Memoirs of a Highland Lady* (1898). Brewster is seen as a model Presbyterian by William Cochran, 'Sir David Brewster: an outline biography', in Morrison-Low and Christie, *Martyr* where Cochran also quotes Brougham's appreciation of the scientist from Margaret Maria Gordon, *The Home Life of Sir David Brewster* (1869).

Talbot's frustration with the camera lucida is recorded in Steve Edwards, 'The dialectics of skill in Talbot's dream world', in *History of Photography*, vol. 26, no. 2, summer (2002). Brewster's enthusiasm for 'numerous beautiful specimens' of photogenic drawing is recorded in the minutes of the St Andrews Literary and Philosophical Society, 1 July 1839, quoted in A. D. Morrison-Low, 'Brewster, Talbot and the Adamsons' – see details above, this chapter. In the same article, Brewster's admission of failure with calotypes is quoted from his letter to Talbot, 26 July 1841 (NMPFT 137-4885). Also in that article, Brewster on Adamson's plan to set up in photography is quoted from his letter to Talbot, 15 August 1842 (NMPFT 137-4905). Hill on Adamson's 'youthful haunt' is in his letter to Henry Bicknell, 17 January 1849 (MS in George Eastman House collection, Rochester, New York).

Chapter 5   At a stroke of the pen

Margaret Oliphant imagined the Disruption scene in her *Chalmers*. The view of Edinburgh by (the other) John Knox can be seen in the Scottish National Portrait Gallery, and Hill's early Disruption sketches are in the Scottish National Gallery archive. Details of the Oil Gas Company at Tanfield can be found in the company's *Prospectus* (1824) and Tom R. Cameron's paper 'A history of gas manufacture in Edinburgh' (1951), both seen in Edinburgh Central Library.

The church historian who approved of the Forty Thieves is J. H. S. Burleigh in his *Church History*. 'Then cometh the blessing …' is from Hill's *Historical Picture* pamphlet. The 'eminent Free Church man' exalted by proceedings at Tanfield was Dr W. Garden Blaikie, quoted in G. N. M. Collins, *The Heritage of Our Fathers* (Knox Press, 1974). The 'less exalted' author is John Cunningham, who wrote a *Church History of Scotland* (1882).

Chapter 6   A message carved in stone

Dull devotions in Kiltearn church, and the Covenanter's headstone outside, were described by Hugh Miller in *My Schools and Schoolmasters* (1854). Roddy Simpson directed me to the stone in Calton Cemetery, Edinburgh, beside which Miller posed for the camera.

Sir Walter Scott's lively if ambivalent view of the Covenanting martyrs is portrayed in his *The Tale of Old Mortality*. David Mack's historical note in the Edinburgh Edition of that novel (1993) provides a concise summary of the background to those troubled times. Scott's reference to 'melancholy tales, hard encounters and cruel exactions' occurs in his *Tales of a Grandfather* (1828); and he quoted from the 'simple, but very affecting, narrative' of John Brown's death – which he found in an eighteenth-century life of Alexander Peden – in a note to the ballad 'The Battle of Bothwell Brig' in his *Minstrelsy of the Scottish Border* (1802–3).

The view of Wilkie as 'the most influential artist of his day' is in Macmillan, *Scottish Art*. Charles Greville's comments on Brougham are from *Greville's England: Selections from the Diaries of Charles Greville 1818–1860*, edited by Christopher Hibbert (Folio, 1981) ('Hibbert, *Greville*').

The launch of the *Witness* and a visit to the editorial office is described in Robert Rainy and James Mackenzie, *Life of William Cunningham DD* (1871). Circulation statistics are given in James A. Secord, *Victorian Sensation: The Extraordinary Publication, Reception, and Secret Authorship of Vestiges of the Natural History of Creation* (University of Chicago Press, 2000); see also R. M. W. Cowan, *The Newspaper in Scotland* (1946). The singular influence of Miller and the *Witness* in the church controversy is noted by Donald Macleod in 'Hugh Miller, the Disruption and the Free Church of Scotland', in Shortland, *Controversies*.

Chapter 7   Hey, Johnny Hope (a reel)

Five dense columns of print in the *Witness*, 27 January 1841, recount the near-riotous events at Marnoch. For the Culsamond episode, see Buchanan, *The Ten Years' Conflict* (1854). It was Buchanan who cast John Hope as 'author of the Disruption'.

Cockburn's comments on 'our high-pressure Dean' are quoted in Stevenson, *Personal Art*, from *Some Letters of Lord Cockburn*, edited by Harry A. Cockburn (1932). Candlish's new brick church was described in the *Witness*, 17 May 1843.

Chapter 8   The greatest living Scotchman

Cockburn quotations are from his *Memorials of his Time* (1856). Carlyle's two-edged reminiscences of Chalmers appear in the entry on Chalmers in the *Dictionary of National Biography* (1908 edition). The Chalmers journal entries are taken from Hanna, *Memoirs*. Hugh Miller's early impressions of Chalmers as a romantic are conveyed in *My Schools and Schoolmasters*.

In 'Thomas Chalmers: then and now' (Cheyne, *Essays*), A. C. Cheyne quotes Wilberforce on Chalmers lecturing, and Hazlitt on Chalmers in the pulpit; and in the same collection Owen Chadwick, in 'Chalmers and the state', cites Chalmers bemused by Coleridge. For the daughter's 'rapture' on the same occasion, see *Letters and Journals of Anne Chalmers edited by her daughter* (Matilda Grace Hanna) (privately printed, 1922). Nathaniel Carter's description of Chalmers in action is quoted by John McCaffrey, 'The life of Thomas Chalmers' (Cheyne, *Essays*); in the same collection, Mary T. Furgol, 'Chalmers and poor relief', quotes the young Chalmers anticipating days of leisure.

The 'oxhead soup or pork broth' dilemma is recounted in Robert Chambers, *A Biographical Dictionary of Eminent Scotsmen* (1870). Glasgow slum scenes are reported by Alexander Brown (the Shadow) in *Midnight Scenes and Social Photographs, being sketches of the life in the streets, wynds and dens of the city* (1858), reprinted by Glasgow University Press (1976) with introduction by John F. McCaffrey; those in Edinburgh are by George Bell in *Day and Night in the Wynds of Edinburgh* (1849). Guthrie's image of 'Hindoos' in College Wynd is from *The Autobiography of Thomas Guthrie, DD and memoir by his sons*, David K. and Charles J. Guthrie (1875). G. M. Young described the 'ghastly lives' of slum-dwellers in his *Portrait of an Age* (Oxford University Press, 1936).

For an analysis of the St John's experiment, see A. C. Cheyne, 'Thomas Chalmers: then and now', in Cheyne, *Essays*, where Thomas Duncan's aphorism on education is repeated. In the same collection, John McCaffrey, in 'The life of Thomas Chalmers', quotes Duncan on Chalmers' supposed view on aristocratic generosity. It was Sara Stevenson in her *Hill and Adamson's 'Fishermen and Women of the Firth of Forth'* (Scottish National Portrait Gallery, 1991) who saw Newhaven as a pattern of Chalmers' ideal society. Dr John Adamson's report on sanitary conditions in St Andrews, from which I quote, is discussed by Graham Smith in 'John Adamson, sanitary reform and the St Andrews fishing community', *History of Photography*, vol. 25, no. 2 (2001). See *Acts 1:8* for the injunction to bear witness 'in Jerusalem, and in all Judaea'.

Chapter 9   Garden sittings by appointment

For a comprehensive guide to Hill and Adamson calotype negatives and salt prints in the Scottish National Portrait Gallery collection, see Stevenson, *Catalogue*. Another significant collection of their work is in Glasgow University Library Special Collections.

Miller appraised the calotype in 'The two prints', *Witness*, 24 June 1843. Brewster's observation of crowds at the Rock House studio occurs in his letter to Talbot, 3 July 1843 (NMPFT 1937-4926), quoted in Morrison-Low, 'Brewster, Talbot and the Adamsons'. Hill's duplicated invitation to sit for a portrait (New College Library, Edinburgh) is quoted in Stevenson, *Personal Art*, as is James Good Tunny's observation of the photographers in his 'Early reminiscences of photography' in the *British Journal of Photography*, no. 12 (November 1869). John Harden's eyewitness accounts of sessions at Rock House are from Daphne Foskett, *John Harden of Brathay Hall* (Abbot Hall Art Gallery, Kendal, 1974) ('Foskett, Harden'.)

Chapter 10   Through a lens, brightly

I have benefited from the wealth of technical and analytical detail on early photography, particularly Hill and Adamson's, in Larry J. Schaaf, 'Science, art and talent', first published in *History of Photography*, vol. 27, no. 1 (2003), and reprinted a special number of the journal *Studies in Photography* (Scottish Society for the History of Photography, 2003); also in the same issue of *Studies in Photography*, Mike Ware, 'On the stability of Robert Adamson's salted paper prints', and K. Eremin, J. Tate and J. Berry, 'On the chemistry of John and Robert Adamson's salted paper prints and calotype negatives'.

Harden on 'the splendid discovery called Calotype' is quoted in Foskett, *Harden*. The 'most thorough and careful washing' is prescribed in an article on photography (probably by John Adamson) in Chambers' *Information for the People* (1857); this is discussed in Ware, 'Stability of prints' (details above, this chapter); Thomas Rodger's 1855 letter to the British Association is in the Mitchell Library, Glasgow – see A. D. Morrison-Low, 'Dr John Adamson and Thomas Rodger', in *Photography 1900: The*

Edinburgh Symposium (1994). The range of cameras used by Hill and Adamson is discussed in Stevenson, *Personal Art*.

Hill admitted ignorance of technicalities in a letter to David Roberts, 14 March 1845, quoted in Stevenson, *Personal Art*. James Nasmyth's jocular enquiry about Miss Mann occurs in his letter to Hill, 27 March 1844 (Royal Observatory, Edinburgh); Hill described the funeral of Adamson in a letter to Joseph Noel Paton, 18 January 1848 (NLS, Acc. 11315), both quoted in Stevenson, *Personal Art*.

Chapter 11   Flittings

Dr Guthrie's sombre forecast on the inevitability of secession is recorded in Thomas Brown, *Annals of the Disruption* (1884), a key source for this chapter. Hugh Miller yarned of John Swanson afloat and ashore in his *Cruise of the Betsey*.

Chapter 12   Kirk without a steeple

Brown's *Annals* is again an essential source; the three *Reports from the Select Committee of the House of Commons on the Refusal of Sites for Churches* (1847) are also important.

I studied *Illustrations of the Principles of Toleration* (1846) in the National Library of Scotland. Hugh Miller described a damp church service on Eigg in *Cruise of the Betsey*. Stevenson in *Personal Art* mentions Hill's fund-raising illustration for the floating kirk.

Chapter 13   Dreams and visions

Hill's description of his frontispiece to *The Land of Burns* is quoted at length by Murdo Macdonald in his "'A somewhat bold capriccio": D. O. Hill's title page vignette', in McKenzie and Thorp, *Studies*. Burns passages are quoted from *The Canongate Burns*, edited by Andrew Noble and Patrick Scott Hogg (Canongate, 2001).

Karl Miller discusses residual belief in fairies and their kind in his *Electric Shepherd: A Likeness of James Hogg* (Faber, 2003).

'Hear me, auld Hangie' is from Burns' 'Address to the Deil'. 'It makes one shudder …': Chalmers' apocalyptic words are from his *Posthumous Works*, quoted by John Roxburgh in 'Chalmers' theology of mission' (Cheyne, *Essays*). Welsh's despairing prayer, 'Oh, I am backward', is in Wylie, *Worthies*. See also John Hedley Brooke, 'Like minds: the God of Hugh Miller', in Shortland, *Controversies*.

Chapter 14   The king is dead

The death and funeral of Thomas Chalmers were extensively covered in the *Witness* (3 June and 5 June, 1847). The 'present-day Free Kirk leader' quoted is Donald Macleod, 'Hugh Miller, the Disruption and the Free Church of Scotland', in Shortland, *Controversies*. For more on Candlish and Miller, see David Robb, 'Stand and unfold yourself: my schools and schoolmasters', also in Shortland, *Controversies*. Chalmers' life as 'a story of failure' is the verdict of A. C. Cheyne, 'Thomas Chalmers: then and now', in Cheyne, *Essays*.

Chapter 15   A shot in the dark

George Rosie's *Hugh Miller* is a good starting point for the study of this troubled genius. Lynn Barber's *The Heyday of Natural History* (1980) sets Miller the geologist in context. Among many contributions to the Cromarty conference 'Celebrating the Life and Times of Hugh Miller' (Borley,

Celebrating), I found Christopher Harvie on 'Hugh Miller and the Scottish crisis', Edward J. Cowan on 'Miller's tale: narrating history and tradition', and Elizabeth Sutherland on 'My Lydia and the women of Cromarty' particularly useful; also essays by Simon J. Nell, Nigel H. Trewin and Michael Collie on the subject of Miller and science; by Ian Maciver on Miller and the foundation of the *Witness*; and by Deryck Lovegrove, Nick Needham and Hugh Cheape on aspects of Miller and the Kirk. Indeed, like Hill when he had trouble identifying everyone in his picture, I could add 'etc., etc., etc.'.

Rosie in *Hugh Miller* quotes John Swanson pointing Miller towards Zion; also the cool criticism of Miller's verse. Lydia's biographer is Elizabeth Sutherland in her *Lydia, Wife of Hugh Miller of Cromarty* (Tuckwell, 2002). Miller's mental state and the attempted cover-up of his suicide is discussed by Roy Porter, 'Miller's madness', in Shortland, *Controversies*.

Chapter 16   So many kent faces

Amelia, the second Mrs Hill, emerges from the shadows in recent research by the photographic historian Roddy Simpson; see also Mike Russell's 'Chipping away the ignorance surrounding Amelia', in the *Herald*, 24 January 2004, and Stevenson, *Personal Art*. Hill's reference to 'gin-horse work' and his determination that the picture 'shall be done', are in his letter to David Roberts, 13 August 1860 (NLS, MS 14836 fo. 165), quoted in Stevenson. Amelia recalled working with Hill when interviewed by Sarah A. Tooley, 'A famous lady sculptor', in the journal *The Young Woman*, August 1895, quoted in Stevenson, *Personal Art*.

The phrase 'St Bartholomew of grouse' is from *Letters of John Brown*, edited by his son and D. W. Forrest (1909) and quoted in Stevenson, *Personal Art*; also quoted there is the guest who 'got on like gunpowder', from *The Letters of John Stuart Blackie to his Wife*, edited by A. Stodart Walker (1909).

The *Scotsman* reported its sneak preview of the picture on 1 June 1864, and on the finished work ('it is alive and arrests') on 24 May 1866.

Chapter 17   Who'll buy?

The context of Hill's great painting and the likely influences on it (including Wilkie) are discussed by Macmillan, *Scottish Art* and Stevenson, *Personal Art*. Goya's *Junta* is illustrated in Robert Hughes, *Goya* (Harvill Press, 2003).

Sir George Harvey's valuation and defence of the picture and the details of its subsequent sale are in Brydall, *Art in Scotland*, as is Sam Bough's sarcastic response to it. 'I thought you a little crazy' – Charles Heath Wilson in a letter to Hill, April 1845 (MS, RSA), cited in Stevenson, *Personal Art*, in which Stevenson also quotes Professor Stuart Blackie's view of the picture as a 'great mistake' (John Stuart Blackie, *Notes of a Life*, edited by A. Stodart Walker (1910). The Heinrich Schwarz verdict is from his *David Octavius Hill, Master of Photography*, translated by Helene E. Fraenkel (1932), quoted in Stevenson, *Personal Art*. Helmut Gersheim referred to 'misspent labour' in his David Octavius Hill memorial lecture, printed in *Creative Camera* (1971). 'The most impressive bad painting' is the verdict of David and Francina Irwin, *Scottish Painters at Home and Abroad 1700–1900* (1975), quoted in Rodger, *Mr Hill*. Sara Stevenson's verdict on the unwisdom of Hill's use of photography as a model for his painting occurs in her essay on 'David Octavius Hill and the use of photography as an aid to painting', *History of Photography*, vol. 15 (1991).

Clarkson Stanfield's praise of the calotypes in John M. Gray, 'The early history of photography', is quoted in Andrew Eliot, *Calotypes by D. O. Hill and Robert Adamson* (1928) and cited in Stevenson, *Personal Art*. The present-day critic writing of 'Raeburnesque effects' is Julie Lawson, 'The continuum of realism: photography's beginning', in *Light from the Dark Room* (National Galleries of Scotland, 1995). In the same compilation, in an essay also entitled 'Light from the dark room', Sara Stevenson quotes Brewster's dyspeptic comments on the supposed flaws of calotype photography, which he made in a 'Review of the progress of photography' in the *North British Review* (1847). Brewster's assertion that there is 'no poetry in the pencil of the sun' in his 1856 presidential address to the Photographic Society of Scotland is quoted by Stevenson in *Personal Art*. Hill's defence of calotypes as 'the imperfect work of a man' is quoted in Stevenson, *Personal Art*, from his letter to Henry Bicknell, 17 January 1849, MS in the George Eastman House Collection.

Hill's rueful comment on seeing the Delaroche painting, made in his letter to Joseph Noel Paton (NLS, Acc. 11315), is quoted in Stevenson, *Personal Art*. Duncan Macmillan referred to Wilkie's *Chelsea Pensioners* in his *Scottish Art*. I quote Greville on Wilkie's *First Council* from Hibbert, *Greville's England*. Hughes on 'mystery' in the *Junta* picture is from his *Goya*.

Chapter 18   The artist in his element

Charles Lee's debt to Hill and Adamson is discussed in *The Golfers: The Story Behind the Painting* (National Galleries of Scotland, 2002). Brian Thom McQuade revealed the link between Lavery and the photographer James Craig Annan in a lecture to members of the Glasgow Art Club, printed as *Glasgow Art Club: The First Ten Years* (2003). I am indebted to Edna Robertson for alerting me to this. Hill's 'romantic and poetic constitution of mind' was recalled by James Nasmyth in his *Autobiography* (1891). Duncan Macmillan defends Hill's painterliness in 'The Disruption Painting' (McKenzie and Thorp, *Studies*). Brydall, *Art in Scotland*, quoted Hill's anonymous newspaper obituarist.

Hill's picture in its Presbytery Hall setting is described and illustrated in William S. Anderson, *A Guide to the Free Church of Scotland College and Offices* (Knox Press, 1994).

The quotation in Chapter 17 from *Goya* by Robert Hughes, published by the Harvill Press, is reprinted by permission of the Random House Group Ltd. Quotations from *Hugh Miller and the Controversies of Victorian Science*, edited by Michael Shortland (1996), are by permission of Oxford University Press.

Acknowledgements

Among those who helped me in the preparation of this book, I am particularly grateful to William S. Anderson, former curator of the Free Church of Scotland Theological College and caretaker of its offices in Edinburgh, who acted as my guide to the Disruption Painting and gave me the benefit of his considerable knowledge of the work and its background; and to the photographic historian and photographer Roddy Simpson, who gave me invaluable insights into – and a demonstration of – the photographic techniques of Hill and Adamson. Robin H. Rodger, Principal Officer, Fine and Applied Arts at Perth Museum and Art Gallery, explained Hill's use of lithography and showed me examples of his work, including a set of his *Sketches of Scenery in Perthshire*. David Weston, Keeper of Special Collections at Glasgow University Library, gave essential advice in the matter of the Hill and Adamson calotypes. My appreciation of the early Free Kirk, its ways and beliefs, was greatly enhanced in discussion with the Rev. William D. Graham, lecturer in church history at the Free Church college, Edinburgh. My thanks also go to the many others who helped in a multitude of ways.

Index